Understanding and Mastering
The Bluebook

Understanding and Mastering
The Bluebook

A Guide for Students and Practitioners

Linda J. Barris

CAROLINA ACADEMIC PRESS

Durham, North Carolina

Library of Congress Cataloging-in-Publication Data

Barris, Linda J.
  Understanding and mastering The Bluebook : a guide for students and practitioners / by
Linda J. Barris.
     p. cm.
  Includes index.
  ISBN 13: 978-1-59460-365-5 (alk. paper)
  ISBN 10: 1-59460-365-0 (alk. paper)
  1. Citation of legal authorities--United States. 2. Annotations and citations (Law)--United
States. I. Title.
  KF245.B37 2007
  808'.027--dc22   2007016474

Carolina Academic Press
700 Kent St.
Durham, NC 27701
Telephone (919) 489-7486
Fax (919) 493-5668
www.cap-press.com

This book is published as a guide to the rules of legal citation set forth in *The Bluebook: A Uniform System of Citation,* Eighteenth Edition, copyright 2005 by The Columbia Law Review Association, The Harvard Law Review, the University of Pennsylvania Law Review, and The Yale Law Journal. *The Bluebook* is published by The Harvard Law Review Association, Gannett House, 1511 Massachusetts Avenue, Cambridge, MA 02138.

Printed in the United States of America

Contents

Understanding and Mastering
The Bluebook

1 Getting Started

This guidebook is designed to help you learn to use *The Bluebook*, but it is not – and is not meant to be – a substitute for *The Bluebook* itself. The citation forms described in this guide are basic forms only. As you will learn, there are many exceptions to the basic rules, and there is simply no substitute for cracking open *The Bluebook* and deciphering the rules.

Before embarking on a study of the *Bluebook* rules, it is important to understand the purpose behind the rules. The purpose is twofold: (1) to indicate to the reader that you are relying upon authority, and (2) to provide a quick way for the reader to locate the authority you relied upon.

For example if you state a rule of law, the reader will want to know where you found that rule of law. Did it come from a case, and if so, which one? Did it come from a statute, and if so, which one? Or did you simply pull it out of thin air? If you do not provide a citation, the reader will assume the latter – that you pulled it out of thin air. Of course this is the last thing you want your reader to assume, since law is based on *authority*, not wishful thinking.

The abbreviations and conventions mandated by *The Bluebook* are intended to help the reader quickly locate the authority. There are literally millions of different sources that a legal writer can refer to including cases, statutes, treatises, and legal articles. Pity the poor lawyer or judge trying to find an authority cited in a document if every writer adopted his or her own citation method. *The Bluebook* is designed to provide a system of citation so that everyone's citations are similar (note that *The Bluebook*'s subtitle refers to a "uniform system" of citation). While *The Bluebook* may seem confusing at first, just keep in mind the confusion that would result if there was no "uniform system."

Important Note

Throughout this guide certain conventions have been employed:

- ● Indicates a Basic Rule applicable to the citation.

- ☞ Points to a tip or explanatory information about a particular rule, or an illustration of the rule under discussion.

- ◆ Indicates that *The Bluebook* allows alternatives, or customary practice may deviate from the *Bluebook* rules. As a practicing lawyer, your employer will have a preference as to which alternative to use. Just as you would check with your employer and adopt your employer's preferred style, you should follow your instructor's preferred style.

> ☞ Many of the examples in this guide use **boldface type** to illustrate the rules.
> DO NOT USE BOLDFACE IN ANY PART OF YOUR CITATIONS.

Important Note: This guide follows the 18th edition of *The Bluebook*. Make sure your copy of *The Bluebook* is the 18th edition.

A. *Bluebook* Organization

Take a few minutes to get familiar with the information in *The Bluebook* and how that information is organized. *The Bluebook* is simply a book of rules governing citation to various authorities. A quick trip through *The Bluebook* will show that there are thousands of rules. To help users find the rules applicable to a particular authority being cited, *The Bluebook* provides tools to help you find the appropriate rules. The following charts show the general organization of *The Bluebook*.

The Rules

The Bluepages Pages 3–43 • Also known as the **Practitioners' Notes** • Rules found in the Bluepages begin with "B."	This section translates the Rules of Citation found in the White Pages into the citation form used by practicing lawyers. This is further explained on the following page.
The Rules of Citation Pages 45–192 • Also known as the **White Pages** • Rules found in the White Pages have no prefix.	This section gives the general rules that are applicable to all citations. These rules need to be translated into Practitioners' Style by using the Bluepages.
The Tables Pages 193–379 • Tables are identified by "T."	This section provides information on how to cite primary authority from specific jurisdictions (e.g., Table 1), and abbreviations for terms frequently encountered in legal citation (e.g., Tables 6 and 12).

The Tools

Table of Contents	Pages vii–xiv	For a **general** rule, start here. ***Example:*** "How do I cite cases?"
Index	Pages 381–415	For a **specific** rule, start here. ***Example:*** "How do I cite a concurring opinion?"
Quick Reference: Law Review Footnotes (inside front cover)		Use this reference only if you are writing a *law review article*.
Quick Reference: Court Documents and Legal Memoranda (inside back cover)		Use this reference to quickly find the general form for Practitioners' Style citations, and as a cross-reference to the controlling White Pages rule.
Quick Index (Back Cover)		The quickest way find the general rules. Also contains a list of the Tables.

B. Practitioners' Style

The Bluebook rules found in the White Pages are designed to guide writers of law review articles. Law review articles are authored by upper division law students, law professors, and occasionally practicing attorneys writing on specialized topics. These articles are accumulated and published in volumes called law reviews.

Practicing lawyers writing legal documents such as legal memoranda and trial briefs must adapt some of the *Bluebook* rules applicable to law review articles (found in the White Pages) to a style suitable for use in a law office. These adaptations are called Practitioners' Style and are described in the Bluepages found at the beginning of *The Bluebook*.

This guide focuses on Practitioners' Style. The details of how these adaptations apply to certain types of authorities will be discussed later, but for now, become familiar with one adaptation that applies to every type of authority you will encounter: typeface conventions.

Important Note
When writing memoranda, briefs, or other law office documents, you will always use Practitioners' Style. Get in the habit of checking the rule in the White Pages, then adapting that rule to Practitioners' Style by using the Bluepages.

Typeface Conventions   Rule B13

The Bluebook uses several typefaces for different kinds of authorities. In the Rules section of *The Bluebook* (White Pages), you will see citations in ordinary roman type, italics, and large and small capitals. As a practitioner, you will use ordinary roman type, and either underlining or italics ♦, BUT NEVER Small Capitals.

☞   See page 23 of the Bluepages for additional information on typefaces, and the examples on the following pages.

♦ Important Note
Traditionally, all italics shown in the rules were converted to underlining in citations. *The Bluebook* now permits the use of either. Some practitioners prefer the use of underlining, others prefer italics. Ask your professor or supervisor which typeface he or she prefers.

Reminders
☞   **Always** convert the typefaces found in the White Pages into Practitioners' Style following the typeface rules found in Bluepages Rule B13.
☞   **Never** use small capitals.
☞   **Never** rely on the authority itself for the correct way to cite it. Not all publishers follow the *Bluebook* rules for citation. Use the information from the authority to assemble your citation, but convert that information into correct *Bluebook* (and Bluepages) form.

White Page Rules and Conversions for Practitioners' Style

White Pages Typefaces	Examples of White Pages Typefaces (Law Review Style)	Practitioners' Conversion (Bluepages)
Roman	This sentence is typed in ordinary roman type.	None needed.
Italic	*This sentence is typed in italics.*	Leave in italics, or convert to roman type and <u>underline</u>. ♦
Small Caps	THESE SENTENCES ARE TYPED IN SMALL CAPS. NOTICE THAT THE FIRST LETTER OF THE SENTENCE IS A SLIGHTLY LARGER CAPITAL.	Convert to ordinary roman type. Underline or italicize ♦ as required. See chart below.

Converting Typefaces to Practitioners' Style   Rule B13

These authorities are underlined or italicized ♦	These authorities are NOT underlined or italicized ♦
• Case names • Procedural phrases (e.g., <u>ex rel</u>, <u>in rem</u>) • Titles of books, articles, and other publications • Titles of legislative materials • Introductory signals • Explanatory phrases introducing subsequent case history, or related authority • Cross references (e.g., <u>id</u>., <u>supra</u>)	• Constitutions • Statutes • Rules of Court • Administrative materials • Executive Orders • Case reporters and services • Model Codes • Restatements

Comparison of Law Review and Practitioners' Styles

Type of Authority	How a citation appears following the White Pages rules for citation.	How the citation appears after conversion to Practitioners' Style using Bluepages Rules.
Cases Rule 10	Metzler v. Rowell, 547 S.E.2d 311, 314 (Ga. Ct. App. 2001) ☞ **Case name written in ordinary roman type.**	<u>Metzler v. Rowell</u>, 547 S.E.2d 311, 314 (Ga. Ct. App. 2001). **OR ♦** *Metzler v. Rowell*, 547 S.E.2d 311, 314 (Ga. Ct. App. 2001). ☞ **Retain ordinary roman type, but underline or italicize case name.**
Statutes Rule 12	OHIO REV. CODE ANN. § 2911.01 (West 2004). ☞ **Code title written in SMALL CAPITALS.**	Ohio Rev. Code Ann. § 2911.01 (West 2004). ☞ **Convert small caps to ordinary roman type.**
Books Rule 15	EDWARD E. PEOPLES, BASIC CRIMINAL PROCEDURE 29–30 (2000). ☞ **Author and book title written in SMALL CAPITALS.**	Edward E. Peoples, <u>Basic Criminal Procedure</u> 29–30 (2000). **OR ♦** Edward E. Peoples, *Basic Criminal Procedure* 29–30 (2000). ☞ **Convert small caps to ordinary roman type; underline or italicize book title.**
Periodicals Rule 16	Youngjae Lee, *The Constitutional Rights Against Excessive Punishment*, 91 Va. L. Rev. 677, 682 (2005). ☞ **Article title written in *italics*.**	Youngjae Lee, <u>The Constitutional Rights Against Excessive Punishment</u>, 91 Va. L. Rev. 677, 682 (2005). **OR ♦** Youngjae Lee, *The Constitutional Rights Against Excessive Punishment*, 91 Va. L. Rev. 677, 682 (2005). ☞ **Convert italics to underline or leave in italics.**

♦ Reminder: *The Bluebook* permits the use of either underlining or italics. Some practitioners prefer the use of underlining, others prefer italics. Ask your professor or supervisor which typeface he or she prefers.

C. Citation Placement Rules

Before assembling a citation to legal authority, you must determine two things:

1. Whether a citation is necessary, and if it is necessary,

2. Where the citation will be placed in the text of your document.

The following section will cover the important rules and customs governing the use of citations in practitioners' documents.

1. Is a Citation Necessary?   Rule B1

- **Basic Rule:** Provide a citation for ANYTHING you take from ANY type of authority or secondary source. Cite ANYTHING you take from:

  - Cases, including facts, rules, holdings, explanations, dicta, and any other information or idea taken directly from a case.

  - Statutes, constitutions, rules and legislative sources.

  - Secondary source material, including examples or illustrations, explanations, or commentary about the law.

- **Exception:** The *only* time you can refer to authority and skip a citation is when you are repeating a concept that you have previously discussed.

  ☞ *Example:* The three-strikes rule discussed in <u>Smith</u> applies precisely to our case.

☞ Study the examples on the following page, paying careful attention to when citations have been included.

Caution

If you omit a citation to primary authority, it tells the reader that there is <u>no authority</u> for what you just said, i.e., it's wishful thinking but not the law.

If you use ideas or information from any type of authority or secondary source without citing that source, you run the risk of a plagiarism accusation. Don't tarnish your legal reputation, or ruin your career before it gets off the ground!

Examples: When to Cite

Michael Adams was employed by the National Bank of Detroit when he was mistakenly arrested and charged with making fraudulent withdrawals from NBD. **Adams v. Nat'l Bank of Detroit**, 508 N.W.2d 464, 464 (Mich. 1993). The withdrawals were actually made by another NBD employee with the same last name. **Id.** Adams suffered no physical injuries based on his arrest. **Id.** The court held that Michigan law does not require that the plaintiff suffer a physical or mental injury to sustain an action for false imprisonment; an interference with a liberty interest is all that is required. **Id. at 466.** Furthermore, any intent to confine the person is sufficient, and even an "innocent or reasonable mistake of identity" will not relieve the defendant from liability. **Id.**

☞ Facts from a precedent case; citation is required.

☞ Additional facts from the precedent case; citation is required.
☞ (**Id.** is a form of citation.)

☞ Holding/rule stated; citation required.

☞ Rule stated; citation required.

In our case, Mr. Smith's ten-hour detention interfered with his liberty interest. Although Mr. Smith suffered no physical or mental injuries when he was mistakenly detained by authorities on theft charges, as the court held in the **Adams**, no such injuries are required for a false imprisonment action. The mistaken identity involved in our case will not relieve Shopper's Paradise of its liability.

☞ Refers to authority previously discussed; no citation required when the writer, not the court, is applying or analyzing the law.

NOTE: Citations in this example appear in bold for ease of reference. Do not put your citations in bold.

2. Where to Place the Citation

Rule B2

After determining that a citation is needed, the next step is to determine where to place the citation within your sentence or paragraph. The rules for citation differ depending on whether the citation:

(1) Is in a separate **citation sentence** following a textual sentence (most common);

(2) Is **embedded** within the textual sentence itself, and is an integral part of the sentence; or

(3) Is a **citation clause** placed within the textual sentence, but is not an integral part of the sentence itself.

Examples: Case Citations

(1) CITATION SENTENCE **The citation supports the entire sentence.**	(2) EMBEDDED CITATION **The citation is an integral part of the sentence.**	(3) CITATION CLAUSE **The citation supports only one part of the sentence.**
Before a federally subsidized housing unit may be declared a drug haven, the Residential Drug-Related Evictions Act requires consideration of seven specified factors. <u>Cook v. Edgewood Mgmt. Corp.</u>, 825 A.2d 939, 946 (D.C. 2003).	The court held in <u>Cook v. Edgewood Management Corp.</u>, 825 A.2d 939, 946 (D.C. 2003) that before a federally subsidized housing unit may be declared a drug haven, the Residential Drug-Related Evictions Act requires consideration of seven specified factors.	Before a federally subsidized housing unit may be declared a drug haven the court must consider seven specified factors, <u>Cook v. Edgewood Mgmt. Corp.</u>, 825 A.2d 939, 946 (D.C. 2003), and dismissal is inappropriate if, because of the presence of some of these factors, a jury could find a "legally sufficient evidentiary basis" for concluding that an apartment is a drug haven, <u>Railan v. Katyal</u>, 766 A.2d 998, 1006 (D.C. 2001).

☞ Notice in the **citation sentence and citation clause** forms, (1) and (3) above, the case name contains an abbreviation [Mgmt.] that is not used in the **embedded citation** form. See the chapter on Case Citations for additional information.

☞ Pay careful attention to the punctuation used in these citations, especially the difference between **embedded citations** and **citation clauses**. In citation clauses, the citations are set off from the text by commas. See the chapter on Case Citations for additional information.

Examples: Statutory Citations

(1) CITATION SENTENCE **The citation supports the entire sentence.**	(2) EMBEDDED CITATION **The citation is an integral part of the sentence.**	(3) CITATION CLAUSE **The citation supports only one part of the sentence.**
The possession of a deadly weapon while committing a theft offense constitutes aggravated robbery. **Ohio Rev. Code Ann. § 2911.01 (West 2004).**	According to **Ohio Revised Code Annotated section 2911.01 (West 2004)**, the possession of a deadly weapon while committing a theft offense constitutes aggravated robbery.	Any instrument capable of inflicting death is classified as a deadly weapon, **Ohio Rev. Code Ann. § 2923.11 (West 2004)**, and possession of a deadly weapon while committing a theft offense constitutes aggravated robbery, **§ 2911.01.**

☞ Notice in the **citation sentence and citation clause** forms, (1) and (3) above, a section symbol (§ or §) is used and some words are abbreviated, while the word "section" is spelled out and no words are abbreviated in the **embedded citation** form. See the chapter on Statutory Citations for additional information.

☞ Pay careful attention to the punctuation used in these citations, especially the difference between **embedded citations** and **citation clauses**. In **citation clauses**, the citations are set off from the text by commas. See the chapter on Statutory Citations for additional information.

(1) Citations in Citation Sentences

- **Basic Rule:** When the citation supports the entire sentence, place the citation after the sentence. The citation sentence begins with a capital letter and has a period at its end – it is its own complete sentence.

Example No. 1: Case Citation

Repetition of the same proposition in several jury instructions is generally within the discretion of the trial court and is not reversible error. <u>Wood v. Hulsey</u>, 271 S.W.2d 218, 222 (Mo. Ct. App. 1954).

Example No. 2: Statutory Citation

The Virginia DUI statute provides that it is unlawful for any person to drive any motor vehicle while under the influence of alcohol. **Va. Code Ann. § 18.2-266 (2006).**

(2) Embedded Citations

- **Basic Rule:** When the citation is embedded (incorporated) into the text sentence and forms an integral part of the sentence, provide a citation **without** setting it off by commas.

  ☞ **Exception:** If the citation comes at the end of an introductory phrase, or an independent clause that would ordinarily require a comma, place a comma following the citation. See example 3, below.

Example No. 1: Case Citation

The court stated in <u>Stamathis v. Flying J, Inc.</u>, 389 F.3d 429, 441 (4th Cir. 2004) that the lack of probable cause alone does not infer actual malice, although it does lend support to that finding.

Example No. 2: Statutory Citation

Robbery is defined by **North Dakota Century Code section 12.1-22-01 (2004)** as a theft accompanied by the infliction or attempted infliction of bodily injury upon another.

Example No. 3: Citation at End of Introductory Phrase

In <u>Stamathis v. Flying J, Inc.</u>, 389 F.3d 429, 441 (4th Cir. 2004), the court stated that the lack of probable cause alone does not infer actual malice, although it does lend support to that finding.

Avoiding Awkward Citation Placement: Part 1

A citation embedded in a textual sentence, especially at the beginning of the sentence, is cumbersome and lessens the impact of the point you are making. Whenever possible, rewrite the sentence so that the citation is placed in a separate citation sentence.

Rewritten Example No. 2 or 3: While the lack of probable cause alone does not infer actual malice, it does lend support to that finding. <u>Stamathis v. Flying J, Inc.</u>, 389 F.3d 429, 441 (4th Cir. 2004).

---

(3) Citation Clauses

- **Basic Rule:** When the citation supports only part of the textual sentence, AND the authority is not an integral part of the sentence, set the citation off from the textual sentence by using commas.

☞ This is most commonly encountered when a single sentence is supported by two or more authorities. See Examples 2 and 3, below.

Example 1: Citation Supports First Part of Sentence Only

Although in Virginia the tort of false imprisonment requires the "direct restraint" of physical liberty, **Jordan v. Shands**, 500 S.E.2d 215, 218 (Va. 1998), we do not get to the issue of restraint in our case because there was adequate legal justification.

Example 2: Two Cases Cited in One Sentence

Exigent circumstances permit a warrantless seizure without probable cause to believe that a crime has been committed, **Figg v. Schroeder**, 312 F.3d 625, 639 (4th Cir. 2002), and such circumstances exist when police officers engaged in lawful investigatory functions would be endangered unless they conducted a warrantless seizure, **Michigan v. Summers**, 452 U.S. 692, 702-03 (1981).

Example 3: One Statute and One Case Cited in One Sentence

The use of litigation reports concerning accidents resulting from the failure of a locomotive boiler is statutorily barred, **49 U.S.C. § 20703 (2005)**, revealing an explicit Congressional policy to rule out reports of accidents even though they may have a claim to objectivity, **Palmer v. Hoffman**, 318 U.S. 109, 115 (1943).

Avoiding Awkward Citation Placement: Part 2

Using multiple citations within one sentence can lead to long, awkwardly constructed sentences that are difficult to follow. Whenever possible, split single sentences with multiple citations into separate sentences containing one citation each.

Rewritten Example No. 3: The use of litigation reports concerning accidents resulting from the failure of a locomotive boiler is statutorily barred by **49 U.S.C. § 20703 (2005)**. This reveals an explicit Congressional policy to rule out reports of accidents even though they may have a claim to objectivity. **Palmer v. Hoffman**, 318 U.S. 109, 115 (1943).

Reminder

In the examples throughout this guide, citations are shown in boldface type for ease of reference only. Do not use boldface type in your citations.

Splitting Embedded Citations in Textual Sentences

The Bluebook requires that the first time an authority is cited, a full citation to that authority must be given. If the full citation is an embedded citation, all citation information must be given within the textual sentence. See *Bluebook* Rule B5.3, and the first example, below.

* **Local Practice Exception**: Local practice in some areas allows the use of a "split citation." In a split citation, only the full case name is included in the textual sentence, while the remaining citation information is provided in a **citation sentence** at the end of the textual sentence.
* ☞ **Never use a split citation when two or more authorities are cited in one textual sentence.**

Examples	
Full citation following *Bluebook* **rule B5.3**	The court held in <u>Cook v. Edgewood Management Corp.</u>, 825 A.2d 939, 946 (D.C. 2003) that before a federally subsidized housing unit may be declared a drug haven, the Residential Drug-Related Evictions Act requires consideration of seven specified factors. The court stated in <u>Stamathis v. Flying J, Inc.</u>, 389 F.3d 429, 441 (4th Cir. 2004) that the lack of probable cause alone does not infer actual malice, although it does lend support to a finding that the defendant acted with actual malice.
Split citation, if allowed by local custom	The court held in <u>Cook v. Edgewood Management Corp.</u> that before a federally subsidized housing unit may be declared a drug haven, the Residential Drug-Related Evictions Act requires consideration of seven specified factors. 825 A.2d 939, 946 (D.C. 2003). The court stated in <u>Stamathis v. Flying J, Inc.</u> that the lack of probable cause alone does not infer actual malice, although it does lend support to that finding. 389 F.3d 429, 441 (4th Cir. 2004).

Caution: Before Using a Split Citation

Ask your professor or supervisor if this is acceptable practice in your locale.

D. Spacing Rules   Rule 6.1

The Bluebook requires specific spacing within the citation. **Always** pay very close attention to the spacing in the *Bluebook* examples (and always ignore the spacing shown on the original authority).

- **Basic Rule No. 1:** Always put a space between each word and distinct part of the citation. In the following examples • indicates a required space.

  ☞ <u>Metzler</u>•v.•<u>Rowell</u>,•547•S.E.2d•311,•314•(Ga.•Ct.•App.•2001).

  ☞ Ohio•Rev.•Code•Ann.•§•2911.01•(West•2004).

  ☞ Jamal•Greene,•Note,•<u>Judging•Partisan•Gerrymanders•Under•the•Elections•Clause</u>,•114•Yale•L.J.•1021,•1044•(2005).

- **Basic Rule No. 2: The Adjacent Single Capitals Rule.** In abbreviations, do not use spaces when the abbreviation consists of "adjacent single capitals," i.e., a single letter followed by another single letter. *Bluebook* Rule 6.1(a).

  ☞ **But see** Rule 6.1(a) for exceptions relating to periodical names.

  ☞ Numerals and ordinals (2d, 3d, 4th, 5th, etc.) are treated as single-letter abbreviations for the purposes of this rule.

Examples: Single Adjacent Capitals Rule 6.1(a)

Adjacent Single Capital Letters	Mixed Single & Multiple-Letter Abbreviations
S.D.N.Y. 4 adjacent single capitals.	S.•Ct. 1-letter abbreviation, 2-letter abbreviation.
S.E.2d 2 adjacent single capitals, 1 ordinal.	Mass.•App.•Ct. 4 letters, 3 letters, 2 letters.
P.3d 1 single capital, 1 adjacent ordinal.	So.•2d 2 letters, 1 ordinal.
U.S.C. 3 adjacent single capitals.	N.J.•Stat.•Ann. 2 adjacent single capitals, 4-letter abbreviation, 3-letter abbreviation.

2 Cases

Bluebook **Rules 10 and B5** control the form for case citations. This chapter addresses the following:

A. The basics of assembling a full case citation;

B. The treatment of case names in citations;

C. Publication information for cases;

D. Information about the deciding court;

E. Year case was decided;

F. Short form case citations; and

G. Additional case citation rules.

A. Assembling a Full Case Citation

Court cases are published in print volumes called reporters, and are also available in on-line databases such as Westlaw or LexisNexis. Both print and on-line resources use the same citation system based on the print volumes of cases, so before you can learn to prepare citations to cases, you need to be familiar with the print reporter system.

Court cases are gathered and printed in volumes called reporters, and these volumes are gathered into sets. There are many different reporter sets, but the most frequently encountered are:

State-specific reporters, which cover one specific state, or one court within one state.

☞   E.g., California Reports, Georgia Appeals Reports.

Regional reporters, which cover several states in a region.

☞   E.g., Pacific Reporter, North Western Reporter.

Federal reporters, which publish federal courts' decisions.

☞   United States Reports (Supreme Court decisions).
☞   Federal Reports (appellate circuit court decisions).
☞   Federal Supplement (district court decisions).

A case citation identifies the reporter set where the case appears, the specific volume from that set, and the exact page number where the case begins. Using this information, a case can be quickly retrieved from either a printed volume from the reporter set or an on-line database. A typical full case citation containing this information looks like this:

Fitzgerald v. Caplan, 362 S.E.2d 103, 105 (Ga. Ct. App. 1987).

☞ A typical full case citation will look the same whether the case is retrieved from a print volume of a reporter set, or the on-line version of the same case retrieved from a database such as Westlaw or LexisNexis.

☞ The first time a case is cited in a document, you must provide a **full** citation to the case. Full citations are discussed in Parts A. through E. of this guide. Short form citations, used for subsequent references to the case, are discussed in Part F.

Case citations are not mysterious–they are simply an assembly job using the various component parts of the citation and following the specific rules for each part. A **full** citation must always have parts (1) through (4), as shown below. The following discusses the individual components of the case citation and the rules applying to each. This is an overview only; always check *The Bluebook* for exact rules and exceptions.

- **Basic Rule:** In a full citation to a court opinion, provide the following information:

    (1) Case name, followed by a comma;

    (2) Publication information including the:
       (a) volume;
       (b) reporter name, abbreviated;
       (c) beginning page number; and
       (d) pinpoint page number, if applicable;

    (3) Court information identifying the court rendering the decision; and

    (4) Year of the decision.

Basic case citation components:

```
              (1)           (2a)  (2b)  (2c)  (2d)      (3)        (4)
   Fitzgerald v. Caplan, 362 S.E.2d 103, 105 (Ga. Ct. App. 1987).
```

(1)	(2a)	(2b)	(2c)	(2d)	(3)	(4)
Case Name	+ Volume	+ Reporter Name	+ Beginning Page	+ Pinpoint Page	+ Court	+ Year

Case Citation Components in Detail

(1)	(2a) (2b) (2c) (2d)	(3)	(4)
Fitzgerald v. Caplan, 362 S.E.2d 103, 105 (Ga. Ct. App. 1987)			

CITATION PART	EXAMPLE	BB RULES
(1) Case Name identifies the main parties in the decided case.	**Fitzgerald v. Caplan**	Rules 10.2 B5.1.1
(2) Publication Information identifies the reporter set in which the case can be found.		Rules 10.3 B5.1.2 Table 1
(2a) Volume identifies the specific volume of the reporter series where the case appears.	**362**	Rule 10.3.2
(2b) Reporter Name (abbreviated) identifies which reporter set and series where the case appears.	**S.E.2d** [South Eastern Reporter, second series]	Rules 10.3 B5.1.2
(2c) Beginning page number identifies the reporter page on which the case begins.	**103**	Rules 3.2(a) B5.1.2
(2d) Pinpoint page number (aka pincite) identifies the specific page within the case where the cited material appears.	**105**	Rules 3.2(a) B5.1.2
(3) Court (abbreviated) identifies the court and jurisdiction that rendered the decision.	**Ga. Ct. App.**	Rules 10.4 B5.1.3 Table 1
(4) Year identifies the year the case was decided.	**1987**	Rules 10.5 B5.1.3

Important Note

This discussion covers basic case citation form only. Case citations may require additional information, some of which will be covered later in this guide. Always refer to *The Bluebook* for exact citation forms.

B. Case Names   Rules 10.2.1, 10.2.2, & B5.1.1

(1)   (2a)   (2b)   (2c)   (2d)   (3)   (4)
Fitzgerald v. Caplan, 362 S.E.2d 103, 105 (Ga. Ct. App. 1987).

(1)	**(2a)**	**(2b)**	**(2c)**	**(2d)**	**(3)**	**(4)**
Case Name	+ Volume	+ Reporter Name	+ Beginning Page	+ Pinpoint Page	+ Court	+ Year

- **Basic Rule:** Provide the names of both parties to the litigation according to sub-rules (a) through (k) described below. Separate the parties' names with a "v." and underline or italicize ♦ the entire case name, but NOT the comma that follows the case name.

The following sub-rules apply to case names, and are discussed in detail on the following pages:

(a) Actions and parties cited	(g) Given names or initials
(b) Procedural phrases	(h) Business firm designations
(c) Abbreviation of party names	(i) Union names
(d) "The" as part of case name	(j) Internal Revenue Service
(e) Descriptive terms	(k) Common name of case differs
(f) Geographical terms	from reporter name.

(a) Actions & Parties Cited   Rule 10.2.1(a)

- **Basic Rule No. 1:** Include the last names or business names of the parties to the litigation. If there are multiple parties (i.e., multiple plaintiffs or multiple defendants), use only the FIRST party listed for the two primary parties to the case. Omit any additional parties.

Susan **Tree** v. Sherry **Jones**	☞	Tree v. Jones
Hall and Tate v. **Dressler** and Spatts	☞	Hall v. Dressler
Bronson v. **Carter**, d/b/a Surf Enterprises	☞	Bronson v. Carter
Toby v. Kane v. Physicians Mutual	☞	Toby v. Kane

- **Basic Rule No. 2:** If the case name includes the term "*et al.*" (a Latin term indicating there are additional parties), omit the "*et al.*"

Fitzgerald v. Caplan, ***et al.***	☞	Fitzgerald v. Caplan

☞ See sub-rule 10.2.1(g), discussed below, for the use of given (first) names and initials.

☞ If the case involves only one party, check sub-rule (b) for procedural phrases.

☞ See Rule 10.2.1(a) for additional information on cases involving partnerships, real property, and bankruptcy adversary actions.

(b) Procedural Phrases   Rule 10.2.1(b)

- **Basic Rule:** Include procedural phrases, abbreviated as appropriate, using the chart below, the *Bluebook* rules, and the case itself as a guide. Always underline (or italicize ♦) both the procedural phrase and case name.

On the relation of	☞	Jones v. Alabama **ex rel.** Smith
For the use of	☞	Trent v. State **ex rel.** Pratt
On behalf of	☞	Scott v. Nevada **ex rel.** Darcy
Next friend of	☞	Hossler **ex rel.** Dows v. Barry
In the matter of / petition of / application of	☞	**In re** Brown
Estate of (no adverse party)	☞	**In re** Estate of Grant
Estate of (adverse party)	☞	**Estate of** Smith v. Jones
Ex parte	☞	**Ex parte** Wendell

(c) Abbreviation of Party Names   Rules 10.2.1(c), 10.2.2, & B5.3

The abbreviation rules differ depending on whether the citation appears in a textual sentence, or a citation sentence or clause. Forgotten the difference? Refer to the discussion beginning on page 11 of this guide.

- **Basic Rule No. 1: Textual Sentence Citations:** In citations embedded in textual sentences, DO NOT abbreviate the names of parties, with the following two exceptions:

  1. **Widely known acronyms:**   ☞   FBI, NAACP, and similar.
     Note: There are no periods in acronyms.

  2. The following eight words, except when they begin a party's name:

And	☞	&	Corporation	☞	Corp.
Association	☞	Ass'n	Incorporated	☞	Inc.
Brothers	☞	Bros.	Limited	☞	Ltd.
Company	☞	Co.	Number	☞	No.

   Examples:

   ☞ Pioneers, Limited   ☞   Pioneers, Ltd.

   ☞ The Company Store   ☞   Company Store *not* ☞ Co. Store

- **Exception:** You may abbreviate additional words of eight or more letters if "substantial" space is saved and the result is "unambiguous."

- **Basic Rule No. 2: Citation Sentences and Clauses.** In addition to abbreviating widely known acronyms and the eight words of Rule 10.2.1(c), also abbreviate any word found in *Bluebook* Tables 6 or 10 when the citation appears in a citation sentence or clause. <u>See</u> Rule 10.2.2.

  - **Exception No. 1:** Never abbreviate the name of a state, county, or country if it is the <u>only</u> word in the party's name.

  - **Exception No. 2:** Never abbreviate United States <u>unless</u> it is part of a longer party name.

Examples: Basic Rule No. 2 for Citation Sentences & Clauses

Tables 6 & 10	Colorado Building and Construction Coalition v. Sampson Housing Association	☞	Colo. Bldg. & Constr. Coal. v. Sampson Hous. Ass'n
Exception No. 1	**California** v. Justus & Bolt, Inc.	☞	**California** v. Justus & Bolt, Inc. Not: **Cal.** v. Justus & Bolt, Inc.
Exception No. 2	Walker v. **United States**	☞	Walker v. **United States** Not: Walker v. **U.S.**
Exception No. 2	Harvey v. **United States Department of Defense**	☞	Harvey v. **U.S. Dep't of Def.**

REMINDER: The abbreviations found in Tables 6 and 10 are for use in citation sentences and citation clauses only. For case names embedded in textual sentences, abbreviate only the eight words found in Rule 10.2.1, and widely known acronyms.

- **Basic Rule 3: Plurals:** To form a plural of any word listed in Table 6, add an "s" at the end of the abbreviation.

☞ Authority	☞ Auth.	Authorities	☞ Auths.
☞ Publication	☞ Publ'n	Publications	☞ Publ'ns

(d) "The" in Case Names   Rule 10.2.1(d)

- **Basic Rule:** Omit the word "the" when it **begins** a case name.

☞ **The** Taylor Group v. Jackson	☞ <u>Taylor Group v. Jackson</u>
☞ Bennie **the** Clown v. Sharp	☞ <u>Benny **the** Clown v. Sharp</u>

(e) Descriptive Terms   Rule 10.2.1(e)

- **Basic Rule:** Omit terms that describe a party's capacity, such as administrator, executor, trustee, etc.

> ☞ Union Bank, **Trustee** v. Green   ☞ <u>Union Bank v. Green</u>

(f) Geographical Terms   Rule 10.2.1(f)

Whether a geographical location that is part of a case name is included in the citation depends upon the identity of the party as a private entity or governmental entity. First determine which of the following types of organizations describes the party, then apply the specific sub-rule for that type of organization.

1. A non-governmental entity, such as a private business or organization;

2. The United States government;

3. A state or commonwealth; or

4. A city, town or county.

1. <u>A Non-Governmental Entity Is a Party</u>

- **Basic Rule No. 1:** Omit prepositional phrases indicating the geographic location of the party UNLESS:

  - The omission would leave only one word in the name of a party, or
  - The location is part of the full name of a business or entity.

- **Basic Rule No. 2:** In citation sentences and clauses, abbreviate states and cities according to Table 10.

Examples: Non-Governmental Entities

Basic Rule No. 1	United Tennis Leagues **of the City of Long Beach**	☞	<u>United Tennis Leagues</u>
Basic Rule No. 1 (part of business name) **Basic Rule No. 2** (abbreviate in citation sentence)	Chem-Co Cleaners **of New York**	☞	***Embedded Citation:*** <u>Chem-Co Cleaners of **New York**</u> ***Citation Sentence or Clause:*** <u>Chem-Co Cleaners of **N.Y.**</u>
Rule Inapplicable (no prepositional phrase)	Staten Island Kiwanis Club	☞	<u>Staten Island Kiwanis Club</u>

2. The United States Government Is a Party

- **Basic Rule:** Omit "of America" after the United States. Do not abbreviate United States UN-LESS it is part of a longer name. Rule 10.2.1(c).

  ☞   United States of America v. Smith   ☞   United States v. Smith

  ☞   United States Department of Treasury v. Smith   ☞   U.S. Dep't of Treasury

  ☞ **Reminder:** This rule applies only when the United States government is a party. If the case involves a private party's name, follow the rules for non-governmental entities.

3. A State or Commonwealth Is a Party

When a state is a party to the case you are citing, the application of Rule 10.2.1(f) differs depending on where you will be using the case, and where the case was decided. Pay close attention to the following discussion and look carefully at the examples to determine which Basic Rule you must follow.

State or Commonwealth Parties: Determining Which Rule to Follow

Situation	Examples
Follow Basic Rule No. 1 if: **The case will be cited in a document for use in the *same state* where the case was decided.**	Your law firm is in **Ohio**. You are preparing a memorandum discussing your client's case that is being litigated in **Ohio**. The case you will cite was decided by an **Ohio** court. The **State of Ohio** is a party to the case you are citing. **Follow Basic Rule No. 1.**
Follow Basic Rule No. 2 if: **The case will be cited in a document for use in:** 1. *A different state* from the state where the case was decided; or 2. *Any federal court*; or 3. *Any state*, when the case being cited is a *federal court decison*.	1. Your law firm is in **Kentucky**. You are preparing a memo on an issue being litigated in **Kentucky**. The case you will cite was *decided by an Arkansas court*. The **State of Arkansas** is a party to the case you are citing. **Follow Basic Rule No. 2.** 2. Your law firm is in **Nevada**. You are preparing a trial brief to be *filed in the Federal District Court in Nevada.* The case you will cite was decided by the **Nevada State Supreme Court**. The **State of Nevada** is a party to the cited case. **Follow Basic Rule No. 2.** 3. Your law firm is in **Ohio**. You are preparing a memo that will be used in **Ohio**. The case you will cite is a *United States Supreme Court decision*. The **State of Ohio** is a party to the cited case. **Follow Basic Rule No. 2.**

- **Basic Rule No. 1:** When citing a decision from a <u>state</u> court in a document for use in <u>that same state</u>, and one of the parties is <u>that state</u>, shorten the name of the party to omit the prepositional phrase, and replace the name of the state with the appropriate description: "State," "Commonwealth," or "People."

Examples: Basic Rule No. 1 — State Is a Party

In a brief to be filed in a **North Carolina** state court	☞	Defendant in case to be cited is the **State of North Carolina**	Cite as ☞	Smith v. **State**
In a memo to be used in a **Kentucky** law office.	☞	Plaintiff in case to be cited is the **Commonwealth of Kentucky**	Cite as ☞	**Commonwealth** v. Smith
In a memo to be used in a **California** law office.	☞	Plaintiff in case to be cited is the **People of California**	Cite as ☞	**People** v. Smith

- **Basic Rule No. 2:** When a state is a party to the case, shorten the state's name to omit the prepositional phrase under the following circumstances. Do not abbreviate state names.

  (1) The case was decided by one state's court, but will be cited in a document for use in a <u>different state</u>; or

  (2) The case was decided by a <u>state court</u>, but will be cited in a socument use in a <u>federal court</u>; or

  (3) The case was decided by a federal court.

Examples: Basic Rule No. 2 — State Is a Party

(1) In a brief to be filed in a **Virginia state court**	☞	Plaintiff in case to be cited is the **State of Illinois**	Cite as ☞	**Illinois** v. Smith
(2) In a brief to be filed in a **federal circuit court**	☞	Plaintiff in case to be cited is the **People of New York**	Cite as ☞	**New York** v. Smith
(3) In a memo to be used in a **Utah** law office	☞	Plaintiff in case to be cited is the **State of Utah**, and the case was decided by the **United States District Court for Utah**	Cite as ☞	**Utah** v. Smith

4. A City, Town or County Is a Party

- **Basic Rule:** When citing a case where one party is a city, town, or county, omit the "City of," "Town of," or "County of," retaining just the name of the city, town, or county.

- Exception: Retain "City of, Town of," or "County of" if it is the **beginning** of the party's name.

Examples: City, Town or County Is a Party

Basic Rule	Mayor of **the City of San Diego** v. Smith	Cite as ☞	Mayor of San Diego v. Smith
Exception	**City of Montgomery** v. Jones	Cite as ☞	City of Montgomery v. Jones

(g) Given Names or Initials   Rule 10.2.1(g)

- **Basic Rule:** Omit given (first) names or any initials of individuals. Omit designations such as Jr., Sr., or IV.

- Exception: Retain given names if they are part of a business firm's title.

Examples: Given Names or Initials

Basic Rule	**Henry** Davidson v. **Deborah** Mohr	Cite as ☞	Davidson v. Mohr
Basic Rule	**Arnie** Trapp, **Sr.** v. Howard Barnes **III**	Cite as ☞	Trapp v. Barnes
Exception	**Jim** Smith Trucking v. **John** White	Cite as ☞	**Jim** Smith Trucking v. White
See Rule 10.2.1(g) if a party's name is in a language where the surname (last name) is given first, as in many Asian names; or is of Portugese or Spanish origin and includes multiple surnames.			

(h) Business Firm Designations Rule 10.2.1(h)

- **Basic Rule:** If a company has two terms in its name indicating it is a business, omit one of the terms.

    ☞ Weston Supply **Co., Inc.** ☞ Weston Supply Co. [dropping the extra "Inc."]

    ☞ Preston Brothers **Ltd.** ☞ Preston Bros. [dropping the "Ltd."]

(i) Unions Rule 10.2.1(i)

Union names are frequently complicated. Always consult *Bluebook* Rule 10.2.1(i) when a union or local union is a party, and follow the examples closely.

- **Basic Rule:** Using the name as printed on the case as a guide, include the "smallest unit" that accurately describes the union. If the union is widely known by an acronym, use the acronym initials, following *Bluebook* Rule 10.2.1(c).

    ☞ Include the name of the local union, if applicable.

    ☞ If the union represents several different industries or crafts, include only the industry or craft listed first.

Example: Sheet Metal Workers' International Association Local 15, **AFL-CIO**

    ☞ Textual Sentence: Sheet Metal Workers International Association Local 15

    ☞ Citation Sentence: Sheet Metal Workers Int'l Ass'n Local 15

(j) Commissioner of Internal Revenue Rule 10.2.1(j)

- **Basic Rule:** Shorten to "Commissioner." Abbreviate to "Comm'r" if the citation appears in a citation sentence or clause.

Example: Commissioner of Internal Revenue v. Jones

    ☞ Textual Sentence: Commissioner v. Jones

    ☞ Citation Sentence: Comm'r v. Jones

(k) Common Name Differs from Name in Reporter   Rule 10.2.1(k)

Occasionally cases may be commonly known by a name other than the official name. The common name of the case may be included in parentheses following the case name to aid the reader in identifying the case. Consult *Bluebook* Rule 10.2.1(k) if you encounter any of the following situations:

1. A case is commonly known by a name other than the one appearing in the reporter.

    ☞ Hint: You may learn that a case is known by another name by reading *about* the case in other sources.

2. A case is commonly known by a short name that is different from the name appearing in the reporter.

    ☞ Hint: Again, you may learn that the case is known by a short name by reading about the case elsewhere.

3. A case where both parties to the case are courts (mandamus actions).

4. A single case has made multiple trips through the courts resulting in multiple opinions with the same party names.

    ☞ Hint: Practitioners often number the cases so that it is readily apparent which case is being cited.

    ☞ Howard v. Trent (Howard III)

Important Note

This discussion covers only the basics of case names, focusing on the most frequently encountered situations. Always consult *The Bluebook* for additional guidance.

Reminder: Do not rely on the case itself to show the correct citation form because publishers may not follow *Bluebook* style.

♦ Reminder

The Bluebook permits the use of underlining or italics for case names. Some practitioners prefer underlining, others prefer italics. Ask your professor or supervisor which typeface he or she prefers. Whatever the choice, be consistent; do not underline some case names and italicize others.

C. Publication Information   Rules 10.3, B5.1.2, & Table 1

The second piece of required information in all full citations is the publication information. This tells the reader where to locate the case in the case reporters, and consists of four parts:

(a) The volume number;

(b) The name of the reporter set, abbreviated;

(c) The beginning page; and (in most situations)

(d) The pinpoint page number.

(1)   **(2a)** **(2b)** **(2c)** **(2d)**   (3)   (4)

<u>Fitzgerald v. Caplan</u>, **362 S.E.2d 103, 105** (Ga. Ct. App. 1987).

(1)		(2a)		(2b)		(2c)		(2d)		(3)		(4)
Case Name	+	**Volume**	+	**Reporter Name**	+	**Beginning Page**	+	**Pinpoint Page**	+	Court	+	Year

(2a) <u>Volume</u>

- **Basic Rule:** Provide the volume number of the reporter set where the case appears.

(2b) <u>Reporter Name (Abbreviated)</u>   Rule 10.3.2 & Table 1

- **Basic Rule:** Provide the abbreviated name of the reporter set where the case appears, using Table 1 in the back of *The Bluebook*.

  ☞ Carefully follow the spacing shown in Table 1 for the abbreviated reporter name. Refer to page 16 of this guide for additional spacing information.

☞ The same case may be published in more than one set of reporters. Be sure to cite the CORRECT REPORTER. To determine the correct reporter set, see Table 1 and the following page in this guide.

Important Note

The Bluebook **requires citation to regional reporters for state court cases, unless a jurisdiction's rule (local rule) requires citation to a different reporter set. If you are unsure what the local rules require, ask your professor or supervisor which reporter set to cite.**

Determining the "Correct" Reporter to Cite

In *The Bluebook*:

1. Find the jurisdiction in Table 1.

2. Find the specific court you wish to cite [e.g., Supreme Court, Appellate Ct., etc.].

3. Read the blurb immediately following the specific court's heading. It will say "cite to [reporter name] if therein, otherwise cite to [reporter name]." Some entries may list one reporter, others may list several.

4. The "correct" reporter to cite is the first-named reporter (look for the words "if therein)."

☞ The alternate reporter set is cited ONLY if the case does not appear in the first-named reporter, or if local rules require.

Example: Citing an Illinois Appellate Court Decision

1. Find **Illinois** in Table 1 [page 207-08].

2. Find the court you wish to cite [it is the second group in Table 1, labeled **Appellate Court**].

3. Read the blurb immediately following the court heading:

   "Cite to N.E.2d, if therein."

☞ The correct citation for this example is:

   People v. Walls, **806 N.E.2d** 712 (Ill. App. Ct. 2004).

> THE PEOPLE OF THE STATE OF ILLINOIS
>
> v.
>
> MICHAEL A. WALLS
>
> APPELLATE COURT OF ILLINOIS, FIFTH DISTRICT
>
> 346 Ill. App. 3d 1154
>
> **806 N.E.2d 712**
>
> 282 Ill. Dec. 415
>
> March 19, 2004

☞ Many reporter sets are published in "series." For example, the North Eastern Reporter is published in two series: (1) North Eastern Reporter [abbreviated N.E.]; and North Eastern Reporter, Second Series [abbreviated N.E.2d]. Be sure to cite the correct series.

4. Compare the Illinois entry in Table 1 to the Colorado Court of Appeals Table 1 entry on page 202. The Colorado entry lists several possible reporters you can cite–but the "correct" reporter is the Pacific Reporter [abbreviated P., P.2d, or P.3d].

> ☞ If the case is not published in the first-listed reporter, (i.e., the Pacific Reporter in the Colorado example), you would then cite to another reporter set where the case does appear. In the Colorado example, the second choice is Colorado Court of Appeals Reports [Colo. App.]. If the case does not appear in the second choice, go to the third choice, Colorado Lawyer. Continue down the list until the you find a reporter that published the case.

(2c) <u>**Beginning Page Number**</u> Rule B5.1.2

- **Basic Rule:** Provide the page number where the case **begins** in the reporter volume.

(2d) <u>**Pinpoint Page Number (aka Pincite)**</u> Rules 3.2 & B5.1.2

- **Basic Rule:** For a full citation, always provide the exact page number where the specific material you are citing can be found, <u>in addition to the beginning page number</u>, unless, you are referring to the case in general.

☞ Pinpoint cites are almost always necessary. The only time a pinpoint is not required is when you are referring to a case in general, without discussing any specific fact, holding, rule, rationale, or other material from the case. The majority of the time, you will need to use a pinpoint page number.

☞ If the pinpoint page is the **same as the beginning page**, repeat the page number as a pinpoint. This avoids confusion: If you leave the information out, the reader will assume you made a mistake – not that the page numbers are the same. See Bluepages Rule B5.1.2.

  ☞ <u>Meade v. Sturgill, 467 S.W.2d **363, 363** (Ky. Ct. App. 1971).</u>

D. Court Rules 10.4, B5.1.3, & Table 1

(1) (2a) (2b) (2c) (2d) **(3)** (4)
<u>Fitzgerald v. Caplan</u>, 362 S.E.2d 103, 105 (**Ga. Ct. App.** 1987).

(1)	(2a)	(2b)	(2c)	(2d)	**(3)**	(4)
Case Name	+ Volume	+ Reporter Name	+ Beginning Page	+ Pinpoint Page	+ **Court**	+ Year

- **Basic Rule:** Identify the deciding court in the parentheses at the end of the case citation, following the abbreviations in Table 1 and using the following discussion as a guide.

- **Basic Rule: STATE COURT cases, apply Rule 10.4(b).** Provide the following information for the court that decided the case:

  a. The <u>state</u> where the case was decided, abbreviated as it appears in Table 1, **UNLESS** the identity of the state is obvious from the publication information; and
  b. The name of the <u>specific court</u> where the case was decided, **UNLESS** the case is from the state's highest court.

   ☞ How do you know if it's the state's highest court? Table 1 lists the courts by rank under each state. The highest court always appears first in the table, followed, in rank order, by the state's lower courts.

☞ **Reminder:** *The Bluebook* generally requires citation to the regional reporters for state court cases, meaning you will almost always need to include the state in your citation.

Examples: State Court Cases

STATE COURT CASES		INFORMATION TO PROVIDE IN THE PARENTHETICAL
Fitzgerald v. Caplan, 362 **S.E.2d** 103, 105 (**Ga. Ct. App.** 1987)	☞	Provide both the abbreviated name of the state [Ga.] and the name of the court [Ct. App.] because that information is not apparent from the name of the reporter. The South Eastern Reporter [S.E.2d] is a regional reporter covering several states.
People v. Crittenden, 885 **P.2d** 887 (**Cal.** 1994)	☞	Provide the abbreviated name of the state [Cal.] because that information is not apparent from the name of the regional reporter [P.2d]. Omit the name of the court because this is a California Supreme Court (highest court) decision.
Bee v. Smith, 6 **Cal. App. 3d** 521, 528 (**Ct. App.** 1970)	☞	Omit the state [Cal.] because that information is clearly conveyed by the name of the reporter [**Cal.** App. 3d]. Provide the name of the court [Ct. App.] because it is not the state's highest court. *The Bluebook* requires inclusion of the court name even when that information is readily apparent from the name of the reporter, as in this example.
Crail v. Blakely, 8 **Cal. 3d** 744, 745 (1973)		Omit the state because the name of the reporter [Cal. 3d] indicates the state. Omit the court name because this is a Supreme Court decision, the state's highest court.

- **Basic Rule: FEDERAL COURT cases.** Provide the following information regarding the court that decided the case:

  a. **United State Supreme Court Cases:** Do not place any information in the parentheses other than the year.

     ☞ Your citation will generally be to the United States Reports (U.S.) which publishes only Supreme Court decisions, therefore the court is identified by the name of the reporter. For decisions prior to 1875, see Table 1.

  b. **Court of Appeals (Circuit Court) cases:** Identify the circuit number (2d Cir., 11th Cir., D.C. Cir., etc.) in the parentheses.

     ☞ Your citation will generally be to the Federal Reporter [F., F.2d, or F.3d]. Similar to a regional reporter which includes state court cases from multiple states, the Federal Reporter includes court of appeals cases from all circuits.

  c. **District Court (trial court) cases:** Provide ONLY the name of the district. Do not provide the division within the district.

     ☞ Your citation will generally be to the Federal Supplement (F. Supp., F. Supp. 2d) which publishes district court cases from district courts throughout the country. You must identify the specific district that decided the case in the parentheses

     ☞ See Table 7 for abbreviations for district courts.

Examples: Federal Cases

Court	Citation	Parenthetical Information
United States Supreme Court	Sosa v. Alvarez-Machain, 542 **U.S.** 692, 701 (2004).	Omit the court name because that information is conveyed by the reporter name.
Appellate Court, 9th Circuit	Leaf v. United States, 588 F.2d 733, 736 (**9th Cir.** 1978).	Provide the specific circuit for federal circuit (federal appellate) court decisions.
District (trial) Court, Northern District California	E.C. Ernst, Inc. v. Contra Costa County, 555 F. Supp. 122, 123 (**N.D. Cal.** 1982).	Provide the specific district for federal district court opinions. Abbreviate according to Tables 7 and 10.

E. Year   Rule 10.5

(1)   (2a)   (2b)   (2c) (2d)   (3)   **(4)**
Fitzgerald v. Caplan, 362 S.E.2d 103, 105 (Ga. Ct. App. **1987**).

(1)		(2a)		(2b)		(2c)		(2d)		(3)		**(4)**
Case Name	+	Volume	+	Reporter Name	+	Beginning Page	+	Pinpoint Page	+	Court	+	**Year**

- **Basic Rule:** Provide in the parenthetical the year the case was **decided** (not argued). Omit the month and day.

F. Short Form Case Citations   Rules 10.9, 4.1, & B5.2

Once a case has been cited in full, subsequent references to that case may be shortened using one of two basic short forms:

(1) Id., or

(2) The case name short form.

☞ These two short forms are NOT interchangeable. See the Basic Rules, below, for an explanation of their individual uses.

1. Id.

- **Basic Rule No. 1:** Id. is used to cite to the SAME authority as was cited in the <u>immediately preceding</u> citation. It may be used with or without a new pinpoint cite. Underline <u>id.</u>, extending the underlining beneath the period.
  - If citing to the **same page** of the **same authority**, no page number is necessary.

<u>Id.</u>   or   *Id.* ♦

  - If citing to a *different* page of the *same authority*, use <u>id.</u> with "at" and the new pinpoint page number.

<u>Id.</u> at 572.   or   *Id.* at 572. ♦

- **Basic Rule No. 2:** When <u>id.</u> appears within a citation clause, it is not capitalized. When <u>id.</u> appears in its own citation sentence, it is capitalized. <u>Id.</u> cannot be used in a citation embedded in a textual sentence; use the case name instead.

Example:

> The granting of reduced prison time for good behavior in contempt cases is within the sole discretion of the sheriff, **id.,** and it is unlikely the Sheriff will reduce time in our case. An inmate is not entitled to due process in regard to the denial of such benefits. **Id. at 1037.**

- **Basic Rule No. 3:** If the immediately preceding citation contains <u>more than one authority</u>, DO NOT use <u>id.</u> Instead, use the case name short form.

Example:

> Even when an agreement makes time "of the essence," this provision can be waived by the conduct of the parties. **Wilson v. King of Prussia Enters., Inc.,** 221 A.2d 123, 126 (Pa. 1966); **Paralka v. Grummel**, 127 A. 619 (Pa. 1925). Courts may find the provision has, in fact, been waived by the parties. **Wilson, 221 A.2d at 126.**

♦ Important Note

Ask your professor or supervisor whether underlining or italicizing is preferred for all citations. Be consistent. If underlining is used for full citations, use underlining for short forms also.

---

2. Case Name Short Form

- **Basic Rule No. 1:** When citations to other authority intervene, or the last citation referred to more than one authority, you cannot use <u>id.</u> Instead, use an alternate short form by combining the:

    (1) Shortened case name;
    (2) Volume number;
    (3) Reporter name, abbreviated;
    (4) The word "at"; and
    (5) Pinpoint page number.

☞ Omit all other information typically found in a full citation, including the beginning page number, court information, and year.

(1)	(2)	(3)	(4)	(5)
Shortened Case Name +	**Volume** +	**Reporter Name** +	**at** +	**Pinpoint Page**

- Basic Rule No. 2: For the shortened name of the case, generally choose the FIRST party, the one listed to the left of the "v." Omit the other party.

  ☞ If your document will include citations to two cases with the same name, choose the second party for one or both of the cases to avoid confusion. For example, if your document will include citations to <u>Smith v. Howard</u> and <u>Smith v. Jansen</u>, choose the second name for short form citations for at least one of the cases.

  ☞ The case name may be split from the rest of the citation and incorporated into the textual sentence. See examples in *Bluebook* Rule B5.2, and on the following page of this guide.

  ☞ You may shorten longer names, but only if the result will be clear to the reader. See the <u>Bendix Autolite</u> example below.

Full Citation	Short Form
<u>Duncan v. Townsend</u>, 325 S.W.2d 67, 70 (Mo. Ct. App. 1959).	**<u>Duncan</u>**, 325 S.W.2d at 70.
<u>Bendix Autolite Corp. v. Midwesco Enterprises, Inc.</u>, 486 U.S. 888, 892–93 (1988).	**<u>Bendix Autolite</u>**, 486 U.S. at 891.

- Exception for Frequent Litigants: If the first party listed is a "frequent litigant" choose the other named party for your shortened case name. "Frequent litigants" includes most state and governmental agencies.

Examples: Frequent Litigants

Full Citation	Short Form
<u>State</u> v. <u>Tupa</u>, 691 N.W.2d 579, 581 (N.D. 2005).	**<u>Tupa</u>**, 691 N.W.2d at 582.
<u>United States</u> v. <u>Hudson</u>, 14 F.3d 536, 542 (10th Cir. 1994).	**<u>Hudson</u>**, 14 F.3d at 542.
<u>Dep't of HUD</u> v. <u>Rucker</u>, 535 U.S. 125, 132 (2002).	**<u>Rucker</u>**, 535 U.S. at 128.

Examples of Short Form Case Citations

One Georgia court held that a patient cannot sue for intentional infliction of emotional distress based on "negligent misinformation" when a doctor inserted a diagnosis of cancer on a patient's insurance claim form with the intention to "fit the plaintiff's insurance claim into one of the pre-ordained diagnostic categories considered compensable by her insurance carrier." <u>Fitzgerald v. Caplan</u>, 362 S.E.2d 103, 104-05 (Ga. Ct. App. 1987). The court found that although the physician inserted the words "Determine Extent of Malignancy" in the space on the form designated "Diagnosis of nature of illness or injury," <u>id.</u> at 104, the doctor's act did not fall into the category of misconduct acts which are of an "outrageous or egregious nature," <u>id.</u> at 105.

In applying the rules, the court reviewed and then rejected <u>Stafford v. Neurological Medical, Inc.</u>, 811 F.2d 470 (8th Cir. 1987), a non-binding decision, where the doctor's misconduct was virtually identical to the <u>Fitzgerald</u> case, but the nature of the claims was different. In <u>Stafford</u>, the plaintiff stated an additional claim based upon negligence and recovered on that basis, <u>id.</u> at 475, while the present case was founded solely on a claim of intentional infliction of emotional distress, <u>Fitzgerald</u>, 362 S.E.2d at 105. The court concluded that claiming intentional infliction of emotional distress based on mere "negligent information" is a contradiction in terms. <u>Id.</u>

☞ **Case 1:** First mention of <u>Fitzgerald</u>; use full cite.

☞ **Case 1**: No intervening cite, new page; use <u>id.</u> with new pinpoint page number.

☞ **Case 1**: No intervening cite, new page; use <u>id.</u> with new page number.

☞ **Case 2:** First mention of <u>Stafford</u>; use full cite.

☞ **Case 2:** No intervening cite, new page number; use <u>id.</u> with new page number. Note how the case name is incorporated into text sentence.

☞ **Case 1**: Intervening cite to <u>Stafford</u>; use case name short form with pinpoint page number.

☞ **Case 1**: No intervening cite, same page; use <u>id.</u> without a page number.

G. Additional Case Citation Rules

The following describes some situations you may encounter when preparing case citations. The special situations covered by this guide include:

1. Parallel citations to two or more reporters;
2. Citing to multiple pages from the same source;
3. Quoting from or citing to a case that quotes or cites another case;
4. Citing dissents or concurrences;
5. Subsequent history for case citations;
6. Weight of authority;
7. Citing cases from on-line sources (star paging);
8. Citing unreported (unpublished) opinions; and
9. Public domain (medium-neutral) citations.

1. Parallel Citations   Rules 10.3.1 & B5.1.3

Many state court decisions are published in two or more sources and you will frequently see citations to cases that provide reference to more than one reporter. These are known as **parallel citations.** For example:

(1st Reporter)   (2nd Reporter)
Fitzgerald v. Caplan, **184 Ga. App. 567, 568, 362 S.E.2d 103, 105** (Ga. Ct. App. 1987).

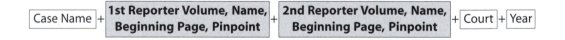

- **Basic Rule No. 1:** Cite only <u>one</u> source unless the local rules of a state require a parallel citation for cases decided by that state.

- **Basic Rule No. 2:** If parallel citations are required, provide publication information for each reporter you must cite, separated by a comma.

- **Basic Rule: Short Forms.** Provide publication information, including pinpoint page references if required, for all reporters you are citing. Rule 10.9(b)(ii).

◆ Check the local rules or ask your professor or instructor if parallel cites are required for a particular document.

Examples: Parallel Citations

Basic parallel citation	Marengo Cave Co. v. Ross, 212 Ind. 624, 630, 10 N.E.2d 917, 920 (1937).
Id. short form	Id. at 634, 10 N.E.2d at 922.
Case name short form	Marengo Cave, 212 Ind. at 638, 10 N.E.2d at 923.

2. Citing Multiple Pages   Rules 3.2(a) & B5.1.2

- **Basic Rule No. 1: Consecutive Pages.** When citing material that spans more than one page, give the inclusive page numbers, separated by a hyphen. Retain the last two digits but drop other repetitious digits.

Examples: Citing Multiple Consecutive Pages

Full citations	Fitzgerald v. Caplan, 362 S.E.2d 103, **104-05** (Ga. Ct. App. 1987). State v. Kwak, 909 P.2d 1106, **1111-12** (Haw. 1995).
Short forms	Fitzgerald, 362 S.E.2d at **104-05**. Id. at **104-05**. Kwak, 909 P.2d at **1111-12**.

- **Basic Rule No. 2: Non-Consecutive Pages.** When citing material found on multiple non-consecutive pages (i.e., skipping pages), give the pinpoint page numbers separated by a comma. Retain all repetitious page numbers.

Examples: Citing Multiple Non-Consecutive Pages

Full citations	Fitzgerald v. Caplan, 362 S.E.2d 103, **103, 105** (Ga. Ct. App. 1987). State v. Kwak, 909 P.2d 1106, **1110, 1112** (Haw. 1995).
Short forms	Fitzgerald, 362 S.E.2d at **103, 105**. Id. at **103, 105**.
The Fitzgerald citations show a pinpoint cite to the first page of the case. See discussion on page 31 of this guide for discussion of pinpoint citations to the first page.	

3. Quoting and Citing Parentheticals   Rule 10.6.2

- **Basic Rule:** When citing a case that quotes or cites to another case, add a parenthetical to the end of the main case citation that includes the citation information for the second case, preceded by the words "quoting" or "citing" as applicable.

Quoting	Citing
"A court properly exercises its discretion if it examines relevant facts, applies a proper standard of law and, using a demonstrated rational process, reaches a conclusion that a reasonable judge could reach." <u>Smith v. Golde</u>, 592 N.W.2d 287, 291 (Wis. Ct. App. 1999) (**quoting** <u>Kerans v. Manion Outdoors Co.</u>, 482 N.W.2d 110, 113 (Wis. Ct. App. 1992).	Under Wisconsin law a default judgment may be entered if discovery statutes or orders are violated. <u>Smith v. Golde</u>, 592 N.W.2d 287, 291 (Wis. Ct. App. 1999) (**citing** <u>Kerans v. Manion Outdoors Co.</u>, 482 N.W.2d 110, 113 (Wis. Ct. App. 1992).
See *Bluebook* Rule 10.6.2 for additional information and examples.	

☞ You must put the parenthetical citation in correct *Bluebook* form, even if it is not in correct *Bluebook* form in the original. Be sure to provide the pinpoint cite to the correct page of the underlying case, even if this requires you to retrieve the quoted or cited case to locate the pinpoint page number.

4. Citing Dissents or Concurrences   Rule 10.6.1

- **Basic Rule:** When citing material found in a dissenting or concurring opinion, indicate that information in a parenthetical at the end of the citation. The parenthetical must provide the name of the judge, followed by a "J." [for judge or justice], and the words "dissenting" or "concurring" as appropriate.

Examples: Dissents and Concurrences

Dissent	The dissent pointed out that the same connections did not exist and as such, a similar level of force could not be supported on the facts. <u>Cotton v. State</u>, 872 A.2d 87, 102 (Md. 2005) (**Battaglia, J., dissenting**).
Concurrence	The district court sees and hears the witnesses, and it is not up to the appellate court to decide whether the witnesses were telling the truth. <u>Beaver v. Mont. Dep't of Natural Res. & Conservation</u>, 78 P.3d 857, 876 (Mont. 2003) (**Warner, J., concurring**).

5. Subsequent History   Rules 10.7 & B5.1.5

Once an opinion is issued by a court, the case is not necessarily over. A party may appeal to a higher court, the case may be remanded to the trial court for retrial, etc. *The Bluebook* requires that some, but not all, of this information be provided in your citation.

- **Basic Rule:** For all cases, provide the subsequent history of the case you are citing if the case was addressed by a **higher** court.

  - Place the subsequent history of the case at the end of the citation following the date parentheses, separated by a comma.

  - Underline (or italicize ♦) the explanatory phrase.

  - Use Table 8 for appropriate abbreviations.

- **Exceptions:** Unless it is relevant to the point you are making:

  - Omit denials of certiorari if a case is **more than two years old.**

  - If the case was remanded to a lower court for further proceedings, omit the history on remand.

  - Omit denials of rehearing.

Examples: Subsequent History

Reversed by a higher court	People v. Hawthorne, 692 N.W.2d 879, 884 (Mich. Ct. App. 2005), rev'd, 713 N.W.2d 724 (Mich. 2006).
Affirmed by a higher court	State v. Thompson, 34 P.3d 382, 386-87 (Ariz. Ct. App. 2001), aff'd, 65 P.3d 420 (Ariz. 2003).
Certiorari denied	People v. Blair, 115 P.3d 1145, 1160 (Cal. 2005), cert. denied, 126 S. Ct. 1881 (2006).
See additional information and examples in *Bluebook* Rules 10.7.1 and B5.1.5.	

6. Weight of Authority   Rules 10.6.1 & B5.1.4

- **Basic Rule:** For case citations, provide information indicating the weight of the authority being cited, enclosed in parentheses at the end of the citation to indicate the precedential value of a cited case. The following information may be included in the parenthetical:

  (a) Information indicating the weight of the authority (e.g., en banc, per curiam, unpublished decision); and

  (b) Information indicating that the proposition cited is not the clear majority holding of the court (e.g., concurrence, dissent, dictum).

Examples: Weight of Authority Parentheticals

Weight of authority	Waters v. Thomas, 46 F.3d 1506, 1512 (11th Cir. 1995) **(en banc)**.
	Collier v. Barnhart, 473 F.3d 444 (2d Cir. 2007) **(per curiam)**.
Non-majority opinion	Mack v. Brazil, Adlong, & Winningham, PLC, 159 S.W.3d 291, 297 (Ark. 2004) **(Corbin, J., concurring)**.
	Troxel v. Granville, 530 U.S. 57, 69 (2000) **(plurality opinion)**.

7. Citing Cases from On-Line Sources (Star Paging)

Court cases are available in both print versions, found in hardbound reporters, and in on-line versions from electronic databases. Although there are several on-line sources available to attorneys, the two most frequently used services are Westlaw and LexisNexis.

The Bluebook **requires citation to the print versions of cases found in the reporter sets.** Many researchers, however, have easier access to on-line versions, or prefer to do legal research using the on-line databases. Some law offices no longer maintain print sets of reporters. This presents no problem to users of most on-line sources because all cases, whether published in print reporter sets or on-line, use the same citation system and researchers can easily retrieve cases from either source.

Although the print and on-line versions contain the same opinion, the on-line versions are not paginated like a book. To provide the pinpoint page number for your citation you will need to determine what page a particular passage would appear on in the printed reporter version. Both Westlaw and LexisNexis make this easy by using a system of pagination, often called "star paging," to indicate the pages in the printed reporter version of the cases.

Follow the instructions below to learn how to convert "star pages" found in the on-line versions from Westlaw or LexisNexis to the print reporter version.

Star Paging

Assume you have an on-line version of the Fitzgerald *case that you retrieved from either West-law or LexisNexis. An on-line copy of the* Fitzgerald *case appears in the Appendix to this guide.*

You wish to cite the following passage in the *Fitzgerald* case:

It is a contradiction in terms to base a claim for intentional infliction of emotional distress on mere "negligent misinformation."

To determine the printed reporter page number for the passage you wish to cite, do the following:

1. Determine which reporter is the "correct" reporter to cite by looking in *Bluebook* Table 1.

2. In the caption of the case, locate the parallel citations.

3. Above the first parallel citation, draw one asterisk; above the second parallel citation, draw two asterisks. If there are additional parallel citations, mark with additional asterisks.

                               *   **

    ☞ **184 Ga. App. 567, 362 S.E.2d 103**

4. Make a note of the number of asterisks assigned to the "correct" reporter.

☞ You have assigned two asterisks to the South Eastern Reporter, the "correct" reporter for Georgia according to Table 1.

5. In the text of the case, locate the passage you wish to cite.

☞ Shown in bold on the second page of the case, right column.

6. To identify the page where this passage appears in the print reporter version, move **backward** in the case until you find the last page number with the number of asterisks assigned to the reporter you wish to cite. This is the print reporter page number you will use for your pinpoint cite.

☞ The passage you wish to cite can be found on page 105 of volume 362 of the South Eastern Reporter print version. A full citation to the passage with a pinpoint cite is:

Fitzgerald v. Caplan, 362 S.E.2d, 103, 105 (Ga. Ct. App. 1987).

It is easy to accidentally pinpoint to the wrong page number by mistakenly using the *nearest* starred page number rather than the page number for the *correct* reporter. In the Fitzgerald example, *568 is the nearest page number for the passage you are citing, but that is the page number for the Georgia Appeals Reports (the "wrong" reporter). To avoid this problem, always double check your pinpoint page numbers for logic. If the beginning page for the case in the South Eastern Reporter is page 103, it is not logical the pinpoint cite would be to page 568.

8. Unpublished Cases   Rules 10.8.1, 18.1.1, & B5.1.3

Cases will frequently appear in electronic sources, including LexisNexis and Westlaw, that are not found in the print reporter sets. These cases are often designated as "unpublished," pending," or "unreported" opinions. They usually lack a citation to a reporter set.

Caution—Citing Unpublished Opinions

Some jurisdictions do not allow citation to unpublished opinions, or do not accord them precedential value. Always check local rules (or ask your professor or supervisor) to determine if citation to unpublished cases is allowed.

- **Basic Rule:** If the case is published in a reporter set, you must cite to the reporter set. If the case is not published in the reporter sets, cite to an electronic database and provide the following information:

  (1) · Case name;

  (2) · The docket number;

  (3) · The database identifier;

  (4) · The database document number;

  (5) · The word "at";

  (6) · A pinpoint cite [an asterisk (*) followed by the database (star) page number];

  (7) · Identity of the court issuing the decision; and

  (8) · The date, including the month, day and year of the decision, using Table 12 for abbreviations.

(1)		(2)		(3)		(4)		(5)		(6)		(7)		(8)
Case Name	+	Docket No.	+	Database ID	+	Document No.	+	at	+	*Pinpoint	+	Court	+	Date

Examples: Electronic Database Citations

This example is a citation to a case retrieved from Westlaw. Notice the "WL" in the database identifier.

(1)   (2)   (3)   (4)   (5)(6)   (7)   (8)
State v. Godfrey, No. COA04-774, 2005 WL 757215, at *3 (N.C. Ct. App. Apr. 5, 2005).

(1) Case Name	☞	State v. Godfrey,
(2) Docket Number	☞	No. COA04-774,
(3) Database ID	☞	2005 WL
(4) Document Number	☞	757215,
(5) "At"	☞	at
(6) Pinpoint Page	☞	*3
(7) Court	☞	(N.C. Ct. App.
(8) Date	☞	Apr. 5, 2005).

This example is a citation to the same case, but retrieved from LexisNexis. Notice the "LEXIS" in the database identifier.

(1)   (2)   (3)   (4) (5)(6)   (7)   (8)
State v. Godfrey, No. COA04-774, 2005 N.C. App. LEXIS 704, at *7 (N.C. Ct. App. Apr. 5, 2005).

(1) Case Name	☞	State v. Godfrey,
(2) Docket Number	☞	No. COA04-774,
(3) Database ID	☞	2005 N.C. App. LEXIS
(4) Document Number	☞	704,
(5) "At"	☞	at
(6) Pinpoint Page	☞	*7
(7) Court	☞	(N.C. Ct. App.
(8) Date	☞	Apr. 5, 2005).

☞ See *Bluebook* Rule 18.1.1 for additional information and examples.

☞ Pay careful attention to punctuation in these examples; be sure to include all necessary commas to separate parts of the citation.

☞ **Reminder:** Use an electronic source citation only if the case has not been published in a print reporter set. Also be sure to check that the case can be used as precedent; see "Caution About Citing Unpublished Opinions," on page 44 of this guide.

Short Forms: Unpublished Cases　　　　　　　　　　　Rule 18.7

- **Basic Rule:** Include the following information:

  (1) Case Name, underlined or italicized ♦, followed by a comma;
  (2) The database identifier;
  (3) The document number, followed by a comma;
  (4) The word "at"; and
  (5) The pinpoint page number.

Examples: Short Forms for Unpublished Cases

Westlaw	<u>Godfrey</u>, 2005 WL 757215, at *3.
LexisNexis	<u>Godfrey</u>, 2005 N.C. App. LEXIS 704, at *7.

9. Public Domain Citations　　　　　　　　　　　　Rule 10.3.3

Some jurisdictions have adopted public domain citations, also known as "medium neutral" citations.

- **Basic Rule:** If a state has adopted public domain citations, an example of that state's required format appears in Table 1, along with the effective date. **Only cases published after the effective date should be cited in public domain format.**

To assemble a public domain citation:

(1) Read Rule 10.3.3 on page 88 of *The Bluebook* to understand what information must be provided in the citation.

(2) Closely follow the example for that specific jurisdiction found in *Bluebook* Table 1.

(3) If the case appears in a regional reporter, that information should be provided as a parallel citation.

☞ **Note:** Table 1 entries show two examples of the form for public domain citation adopted in the specific jurisdiction. The first example shows a citation to a case in general, without a pinpoint cite. The second example shows a citation *with* a pinpoint cite. Notice that the pinpoint cite is to a paragraph number (instead of a page) and is indicated by the paragraph symbol [¶]. Paragraphs may be marked in the text of the case by a "P," as shown in the example below marking paragraph 8 of the <u>Coyne</u> case, but use the paragraph symbol in your citation.

☞ For further information on paragraph symbols, including keyboard shortcuts, see page 114 of this guide.

Example: Public Domain Citations

The Case You Are Citing	Entry in Bluebook Table 1	Citation in Your Document
Gregory Coyne v. Greg Peace SUPREME JUDICIAL COURT OF MAINE 2004 ME 150; 863 A.2d 885 863 A.2d 885 December 14, 2004, Decided [Portions of case omitted.] **[*P8] The court also instructed, as part of its definition of negligence, on several rules of the road regarding operation of snowmobiles.**	"Public domain citation format: Maine has adopted a public domain citation format for cases after December 31, 1996. The format is: " ――――――――――― <u>Case name</u> + date + ME + document number + pinpoint paragraph number, if applicable + parallel cite to Atlantic Reporter, including pinpoint page number.	"The court also instructed, as part of its definition of negligence, on several rules of the road regarding operation of snowmobiles." **Coyne v. Peace, 2004 ME 150, ¶8, 863 A.2d 885, 889.**

3 Statutes

Bluebook **Rules 12 and B6** control the form for statutory citations. This chapter addresses the following:

A. State statutory citations;

B. Federal statutory citations;

C. Citing named statutes;

D. Citing multiple statutory sections; and

E. Short form statutory citations.

Statutes enacted by a legislature are organized, usually by subject matter, into what is known as a "code." States and the federal government publish their codes in multi-volume sets. Many code sets are published in both official and unofficial versions. Official codes are issued by the jurisdiction itself, while unofficial codes are published by independent publishers (often West or LexisNexis). *Bluebook* Table 1 lists the codes available in each jurisdiction.

- **Basic Rule: Code Version.** *Bluebook* Rule 12.2.1 requires citation to the official code "if possible."

    ☞ Law firms and libraries often carry only the unofficial codes because the unofficial sets contain useful editorial enhancements. **If your library carries the official code, you must cite to the official code. If your library only carries an unofficial code, cite the unofficial code.** A growing number of states no longer publish official codes, relying instead on private publishers. No matter the situation, always follow the citation form indicated in Table 1 for the code set you are using.

☞ Citation forms vary depending on whether the citation is to a state or federal statute. ALWAYS consult *Bluebook* Table 1 for correct citation forms for the specific jurisdiction being cited.

A Note About Typefaces

All parts of a statutory citation should be printed in ordinary roman type. Do not underline any part of the statutory citation. Do not use SMALL CAPITALS, even though the examples printed in *Bluebook* Table 1 show the names of code written in small capitals. <u>See</u> *Bluebook* Rule B13.

A. State Statutory Citations   Rule 12

- **Basic Rule:** For a full citation to a state statute, include the following parts, <u>in ordinary roman type</u>, in the format specified by *Bluebook* Table 1 for the jurisdiction:

  (1) Name of the code being cited;

  (2) Section symbol, or the word section spelled out;

  (3) Section number;

  (4) The name of the publisher, but only if citing to an unofficial code;

  (5) The abbreviation for supplement, if applicable; and

  (6) The year of the code.

(1)	(2)	(3)	(4)	(5)	(6)
Code Name	+ § +	Section No.	+ If Applicable: Publisher &/or Supplement Info.	+	Code Year

Examples: Full Statutory Citations

Official Code	*Citation Sentence*	☞	(1) (2) (3) (6) **Iowa Code § 237.9 (2003).**
	Textual Sentence	☞	(1) (2) (3) (6) **Iowa Code section 237.9 (2003).**
Unofficial Code	*Citation Sentence*	☞	(1) (2) (3) (4) (6) **Iowa Code Ann. § 237.9 (West 2000).**
	Textual Sentence	☞	(1) (2) (3) (4) (6) **Iowa Code Ann. section 237.9 (West 2000).**
Supplement to Official Code	*Citation Sentence*	☞	(1) (2) (3) (5) (6) **Iowa Code § 249.3 (Supp. 2005).**
	Textual Sentence	☞	(1) (2) (3) (5) (6) **Iowa Code section 249.3 (Supp. 2005).**
Supplement to Unofficial Code	*Citation Sentence*	☞	(1) (2) (3) (4) (5) (6) **Iowa Code § 249.3 (West Supp. 2005).**
	Textual Sentence	☞	(1) (2) (3) (4) (5) (6) **Iowa Code section 249.3 (West Supp. 2005).**

How to Determine a State's Statutory Citation Form

1. Find the state's entries in *Bluebook* Table 1.

   ☞ For example, to cite the Iowa statute illustrated on the preceding page, find Iowa's entries in *Bluebook* Table 1, page 209.

2. Find the section entitled "**Statutory compilations.**"

3. Read the words following the title "Statutory compilations."

   ☞ Statutory compilations: Cite to Iowa Code, if therein.

4. Immediately beneath the Statutory compilations heading are two columns. The column on the left lists the names of all code sets available in that jurisdiction. The right column shows the citation form for each available code set.

   ☞ **Statutory compilations**: Cite to Iowa Code, if therein.

   • Code of Iowa   Iowa Code § x.x (year)
   • West's Iowa Code Annotated   Iowa Code Ann. § x.x (West year)

5. Copy the citation form shown in the right hand column in Table 1, substituting the section number for the "x" and placing the code year in the parentheses.

   ☞ Be sure to copy the abbreviations and spacing shown in *Bluebook* Table 1 **exactly**, but convert the typeface to <u>ordinary roman type</u>.

The citation form as it appears in Table 1, right column:	The citation as it will be formatted in your document:
Iowa Code § x.x (year)	Iowa Code § 237.9 (2003).
Iowa Code Ann. § x.x (West year)	Iowa Code Ann. § 237.9 (West 2000).

☞ **Each component of a statutory citation is discussed in detail on the following pages of this guide.**

(1) Code Name   Rules 12.2 & B6.1.2

(1)

| Code Name | + | § | + | Section No. | + | If Applicable: Publisher &/or Supplement Info. | + | Code Year |

- **Basic Rule No. 1:** Include the name of the code you are citing, following the form specific to the jurisdiction and code set, as shown under "Statutory compilations" in Table 1.

  ☞ **Reminder:** Cite to the official code "if possible." Cite to the unofficial code only if the official code is unavailable.

- **Basic Rule No. 2:** Abbreviate the name of the code according to Table 1 in citation sentences and clauses only. Do not abbreviate if the name of the code is embedded in a textual sentence.

Examples: Code Name

Citation Sentences and Clauses	**Iowa Code Ann.** § 237.9 (West 2000).
	R.I. Gen. Laws § 11-7-11 (2004).
Citations in Textual Sentences	**Iowa Code Annotated** section 237.9 (West 2000)
	Rhode Island General Laws section 11-7-11 (2002)

- **Basic Rule No. 3: Subject Codes.** Some states divide their codes by subject matter. The subject matter is included as part of the code name. Follow the abbreviation rules described in **Basic Rule No. 2**, abbreviating the subject name as shown in Table 1 if the citation appears in a citation sentence or clause. <u>See</u> Rule 12.3.1(c).

Examples of Subject Matter Codes

Citation Sentences and Clauses	**Cal. Fam. Code** § 3900 (Deering 2003).
	Md. Code Ann., Crim. Law § 2-103 (West 2001).
Citations in Textual Sentences	**California Family Code** section 3900 (Deering 2003)
	Maryland Code Annotated, Criminal Law section 2-103 (West 2001)

(2) Section [§]   Rules 12.9(d) & 3.3

(2)

| Code Name | + | § | + | Section No. | + | If Applicable: Publisher &/or Supplement Info. | + | Code Year |

- **Basic Rule:** Follow the code name with a section symbol (in citation sentences or clauses), or the word section spelled out (in textual sentences). For help creating a section symbol, see page 114 of this guide.

Examples: Section Symbol or Word

Citation Sentences and Clauses	Alaska Stat. § 16.35.200 (2005).
Textual Sentences	Alaska Statutes **section** 16.35.200 (2005)

(3) Section Number   Rule 12.3.1(b)

(3)

| Code Name | + | § | + | Section No. | + | If Applicable: Publisher &/or Supplement Info. | + | Code Year |

- **Basic Rule No. 1: Citing an Entire Section.** Provide the section number for the statutory section you are citing, following the form shown in *Bluebook* Table 1. Leave a space between the section symbol and section number.

  ☞ Many states set off sections by dashes or periods, while others include "title" (abbreviated "tit.") with the section number. Closely follow the format shown in Table 1 for the specific jurisdiction.

Examples: Section Numbers

The citation form as it appears in Table 1, right column:	The citation as it will be formatted in your document:
KY. REV. STAT. ANN. § x.x (LexisNexis year)	Ky. Rev. Stat. Ann. § **187.070** (LexisNexis 2003).
N.J. STAT. ANN. § x:x (West year)	N.J. Stat. Ann. § **9:21-1** (West 2002).
ME. REV. STAT. ANN. **tit. x, § x** (year)	Me. Rev. Stat. Ann. **tit. 36, § 4302** (1994).
ALA. CODE § x-x-x (year)	Ala. Code § **12-15-8** (1999)

- **Basic Rule No. 2: Citing Subsections.** To cite a specific <u>sub</u>section of a statute, provide the section number for the entire statute, followed by the subsection number. Use the original punctuation separating sections from subsections [usually parenthesis or dashes]. If the statute contains no separating punctuation, place the subsection in parentheses.

Examples: Citing Entire Sections v. Subsections

NEVADA REVISED STATUTES
TITLE 12. WILLS AND ESTATES OF DECEASED PERSONS
CHAPTER 133. WILLS, REVOCATION

§ 133.120 Other means of revocation

1.   A written will may only be revoked by:
    (a) Burning, **tearing**, canceling or obliterating the will, with the intention of revoking it, by the testator, or by some person in the presence and at the direction of the testator; or
    (b) Another will or codicil in writing, executed as prescribed in this chapter.

2.   This section does not prevent the revocation implied by law from subsequent changes in the condition or circumstances of the testator.

To cite the **ENTIRE SECTION**	Nev. Rev. Stat. § **133.120** (2003).
To cite all of **SUBSECTION 1** **[discussing all means of revoking a will]**	Nev. Rev. Stat. § **133.120(1)** (2003). Subsection 1 is not separately punctuated in the statute. Enclose the subsection number in parentheses to distinguish it from the main portion of the statute.
To cite to **SUB-SUBSECTION (a)** **[discussing revocation by tearing]**	Nev. Rev. Stat. § **133.120(1)(a)** (2003). Sub-subsection (a) is separately punctuated [enclosed in parentheses]. Add the parenthetical sub-subsection to the end of the subsection number.

☞ **Keep adding sub-subsection numbers as necessary to pinpoint the exact portion of the statute you are discussing.**

☞ **Notice there are NO SPACES between the subsection parentheticals, but don't forget to put a space between the section symbol and the section number.**

Note

DO NOT substitute a dollar sign [$], "at" sign [@], or a capital S for the section symbol—you must use the section symbol. See page 114 of this guide for assistance.

---

(4) Publisher (if Applicable)   Rule 12.3.1(d)

(4)

| Code Name | + | § | + | Section No. | + | If Applicable: Publisher &/or Supplement Info. | + | Code Year |

- **Basic Rule:** When citing to an <u>unofficial code</u>, provide the name of the publisher in parentheses at the end of the citation. If citing to an <u>official code</u>, omit the publisher's name. Follow the examples in *Bluebook* Table 1 for the specific state.

Examples: Publisher

Official Code	Iowa Code § 237.9 (2003).
	N.M. Stat. § 16-2-11 (2002).
Unofficial Code	Iowa Code Ann. § 237.9 (**West** 2000).
	W. Va. Code Ann. § 16-2E-2 (**LexisNexis** 2005).
☞ **Important Note: See "A Word About Publishers" in the next section.**	

(5) Supplements (if Applicable)   Rules 12.3.1(e) & 3.1(c)

(5)

| Code Name | + | § | + | Section No. | + | If Applicable: Publisher &/or Supplement Info. | + | Code Year |

- **Basic Rule:** When citing a statutory section that is printed in a supplement (or pocket part), include the abbreviation "Supp." before the code year in the parentheses at the end of the citation. If you are citing to an unofficial code, include the word Supp. <u>after</u> the name of the publisher.

Examples: Supplements

Official Code	Iowa Code § 237.9 (**Supp.** 2006).
Unofficial Code	Iowa Code Ann. § 237.9 (West **Supp.** 2005).

A Word About Publishers

In recent years there has been a trend toward consolidation of legal publishers. During this ongoing process, some states' hardbound code sets may identify one publisher, while *Bluebook* Table 1 shows a different publisher. Or, the softbound supplement or insert (pocket part) may be published by a different company than the hardbound volume, reflecting a recent change in ownership of the publishing company.

- **Basic Rule:** Always follow the example in *Bluebook* Table 1 for the correct publication information, but substitute the publisher's name appearing on the volume or supplement you are using.

---

(6) Code Year   Rule 12.3.2

(6)

| Code Name | + | § | + | Section No. | + | If Applicable: Publisher &/or Supplement Info. | + | Code Year |

- **Basic Rule: Main Volume.** Place the year of the code in parentheses at the end of the citation (together with any applicable publisher and supplement information). **The year of the code is determined by checking for these dates, <u>in the following order</u>:**

  1. **Book spine:** If a year is printed on the spine of the book, use that date.

  2. **Title page:** If no year appears on the spine, use the year printed on the title page.

  3. **Copyright date:** If no year appears on the spine or on the title page, use the copyright year.

☞ Important Note: The required information is the "code year," not the year the statute was enacted. Code year refers to the year of the latest <u>printing</u> of the code.

• **Basic Rule: Supplements.** If you are citing material contained in a **supplement**, the code year is determined by checking for these dates, <u>in the following order</u>:

1.   **Title page:** If the year is printed on the title page of the <u>supplement</u>, use that date.

2.   **Copyright date:** If no year appears on the title page of the supplement, use the copyright year of the <u>supplement</u>.

Examples: Code Year and Supplements

Citing the main volume of the OFFICIAL Iowa Code.	Iowa Code § 237.9 (**2003**).
Citing the pocket part supplement of the OFFICIAL Iowa Code.	Iowa Code § 237.9 (**Supp. 2007**).
Citing the main volume of the OFFICIAL Iowa Code AND to the supplement.	Iowa Code § 237.9 (**2003 & Supp. 2007**).
Citing the main volume of the UNOFFICIAL Iowa Code and the supplement.	Iowa Code Ann. § 237.9 (**West 2005 & Supp. 2007**).

B. Federal Statutory Citations   Rules 12 & B6.1.1

You may either cite directly to an individual section of the Code, following **Basic Rule No. 1**, or you may cite to the original act if the law you are discussing has a common name, following **Basic Rule No. 2**. Examples of statutes that are known by a common name include the Americans with Disabilities Act, the Homeland Security Act, etc.

• **Basic Rule No. 1: Direct Citations to the Code:** For citations to individual statutes within the United States Code, provide the following information:

(1) Title number;

(2) Name of the code, abbreviated;

(3) Section symbol;

(4) Section number;

(5) The abbreviation for supplement, if applicable; and

(6) The year of the code.

(1)		(2)		(3)		(4)		(5)		(6)
Title Number	+	**Code Name**	+	**§**	+	**Section Number**	+	**Supp., if applicable**	+	**Code Year**

☞ *Bluebook* Table 1 shows the proper form for citations to the United States Code. In general, follow the same rules applicable to state statutory citations, but note the following differences:

1. **Title Number:** Place the title number for the code <u>before</u> the name of the Code;

2. **Name of Code:** *The Bluebook* requires citation to the official code, the United States Code (U.S.C.) "if therein." If the official code is unavailable, cite to an unofficial code.

3. **Section Symbol:** Always use the section symbol when referring to United States Code provisions; do not spell out "section" even when the citation is embedded in a textual sentence. <u>See</u> *Bluebook* Rule 12.9(d).

Examples: Federal Statutory Citations

Citation Sentences and Clauses	42 U.S.C. § 1652 (2002).
Textual Sentences	According to **42 U.S.C. § 1652 (2002)**, the minimum limit on weekly compensation for disability does not apply in computing compensation and death benefits under the Act. ☞ *Notice there is no difference between the citation sentence and textual sentence form of citation to federal statutes; both use the section symbol instead of spelling out the word "section" in embedded citations, as is required in state statutory citations.*

C. Named Statutes   Rules 12.2.1 & B6.1.1

- **Basic Rule: Citation to Statutes with Common Names.** For a full citation to a statute that is known by a common name, provide the official name of the act, followed by all the information required for the specific jurisdiction's statutes according to Table 1.

  ☞ In other words, use all the information described in parts A. or B., above, adding the name of the statute to the beginning of the citation, plus the section number of the original act, if applicable. See examples below, and in *Bluebook* Rule 12.2.1.

Examples: Named Statutes

State	**Sex Offenders Registration Act**, 730 Ill. Comp. Stat. § 150/3 (West 2005).
Federal	**Homeland Security Act of 2002 § 517**, 6 U.S.C. § 321f (2004).

D. Citing Multiple Statutory Sections   Rule 3.3(b)

1. Spanning Consecutive Sections and Subsections

- **Basic Rule: Sections.** To cite material **spanning** more than one consecutive **section**, provide the section numbers, separated by a <u>hyphen</u>. Use TWO section symbols to indicate multiple sections.

- **Basic Rule: Subsections.** To cite material **spanning** more than one consecutive **subsection** within the same section, provide the <u>subsection</u> numbers, separated by a hyphen. Use ONE section symbol (because you are only citing one *section*).

- **Basic Rule: Repetitious Digits.** Drop any repetitious digits that <u>precede</u> a punctuation mark, unless it would cause confusion. If confusion would result, either retain repetitious digits, or include the word "to" to separate the sections or subsections.

Examples: Spanning Consecutive Sections and Subsections

Spanning Sections	Cal. Lab. Code **§§ 6302-6303** (Deering 2003). *Retain repetitious digits not separated by punctuation.*
Spanning Sections	Ohio Rev. Code Ann. **§§ 5307.12-.13** (West 2006). *Drop repetitious digits preceding punctuation.*
Spanning Sections	N.M. Stat. Ann. **§ 31-2-1 to -3** (LexisNexis 2005) ***Not:*** *N.M. Stat. Ann. § 31-2-1-3 (LexisNexis 2005)* *Include "to," in this situation, avoiding the confusion caused by dropping repetitious digits.*
Spanning <u>Subsections</u>	Cal. Lab. Code **§ 6302(a)-(d)** (Deering 2003).

2. Skipping Sections and Subsections (Non-Consecutive Sections)

- **Basic Rule:** To cite material that skips sections or <u>sub</u>sections, (non-consecutive sections), within one title or chapter, follow same rules for "spanning" sections, described above, EXCEPT: Separate individual sections or subsections by a <u>comma</u>.

Examples: Skipping Sections and Subsections (Non-Consecutive Sections)

Skipping Sections	Cal. Lab. Code **§§ 6302, 6305** (Deering 2003).
Skipping Sections	N.M. Stat. Ann. **§ 31-2-1, -5** (LexisNexis 2005)
Skipping <u>Subsections</u>	Cal. Lab. Code **§ 6302(a), (d)** (Deering 2003).

E. Short Form Statutory Citations   Rules 12.9 & B6.2

Once a statute has been cited in full, shorten subsequent references to that statute, or other statutes found in the **same title or chapter**, by using one of two basic forms, described in detail below:

1. <u>Id.</u>; or

2. Repeating the statute's number.

☞ To cite a statute found in a **different title or chapter**, you must give a full citation the first time it is cited.

---

1. <u>Id.</u>

- **Basic Rule:** <u>Id.</u> may be used to cite the same statute as was cited in the immediately preceding authority. <u>Id.</u> may be used alone to cite the same section as the previous cite, or combined with a new section or subsection number. <u>Id.</u> may be underlined or italicized ♦.

Examples: Use of <u>Id.</u> in Statutory Citations

First Full Citation	Okla. Stat. **tit. 3, § 106(1)** (1999).
Citing Same Section and Subsection	<u>Id.</u>
Citing Same Section, New Subsection	<u>Id.</u> § **106(2)**.
Citing Same Title, New Section	<u>Id.</u> § **254.2**.
Citing Different Title	Okla. Stat. **tit. 10, § 83** (1999).

☞ **DO NOT use the word "at" between the word <u>id.</u> and the section symbol and number.**

Reminders

♦ **Ask your professor or supervisor whether underlining or italicizing is preferred for all citations. Be consistent. If underlining is used for full citations, use underlining for short forms also.**

If you underline <u>id.</u>, extend the underlining beneath the period.

When <u>id.</u> appears within a citation clause, it is not capitalized. When <u>id.</u> appears in its own citation sentence, it is capitalized. Do not embed <u>id.</u> as an integral part of a citation sentence.

If the immediately preceding citation contains more than one authority, you cannot use <u>id.</u> Instead, use the alternate short form shown on the next page.

2. Repeating Statute Number

● **Basic Rule:** When a citation to another authority intervenes, including a citation to a statute found in a different title or chapter, use an alternate short form that "clearly identifies the statute" being cited.

☞ The exact form of the citation will vary depending on the form the jurisdiction has adopted. Use the following examples as a guide, and look carefully at *Bluebook* Rule 12.9. You may also use the jurisdiction's practice as a reference; look at how cases in the jurisdiction treat short form statutory citations.

Examples: Reference to Statutory Section

FULL CITATION	SHORT FORMS		
21 U.S.C. § 457 (2002).	§ U.S.C. § 457.	or	§ 457.
Homeland Security Act of 2002 § 309, 6 U.S.C. § 189 (2006).	Homeland Security Act § 189 or 6 U.S.C. § 189	or	§ 189
Okla. Stat. tit. 3, § 106(1) (1999).	tit. 3, § 106(1).	or	§ 106(1).
N.Y. Lien Law § 3 (McKinney 2005).	Lien § 3.	or	§ 3.
Tenn. Code Ann. § 39-13-202 (2006) (Title [39], chapter [13] and section [202])	§ 39-13-202.	or	Customary practice uses all parts, not just section number.

If you have cited to multiple statutes in your document, generally choose the "longer" short form, shown in the middle column, to avoid confusion. If your document, or the discussion in a particular portion of a longer document, cites to only one statute, use the "shorter" short form shown in the right column. When there is <u>any</u> chance of the reader being confused about which statute you are referring to, use the longer version or a full citation.

Important Note

The discussion in this chapter covers basic statutory citation rules only. *The Bluebook* has special rules for citations to repealed statutes, an entire legislative act, individual portions of legislative acts, session laws (for uncodified acts), and named statutes published in scattered sections of the code. See *Bluebook* Rules 12 and B6.1, if you encounter any of these situations.

Examples: Short Form Statutory Citations

Florida statutes are divided into chapters and sections. The first example below shows a citation to Chapter 741, Section 24, subsection 1.

If a minor child "living with the parents" maliciously or willfully destroys or steals property belonging to a school, the school is entitled to recover damages from the parents. **Fla. Stat. § 741.24(1) (2006).** This rule applies to both public and private schools. Id.

☞ First cite to statute; use full citation.

☞ Same section and subsection; use id.

When parents are divorced and the child lives with one parent, application of the statute has been limited to the parent who has primary custody and control over the child. <u>Canida v. Canida</u>, **751 So. 2d 647, 648 (Fla. Dist. Ct. App. 1999).** This comports with the statutory language requiring the minor to be "living with" the parents. **§ 741.24(1).**

☞ Intervening cite to case.

☞ Cannot use id. because of intervening cite. Repeat statute number.

To recover, the school must bring "an appropriate action at law in a court of competent jurisdiction." Id. Recovery is limited to actual damages plus court costs, id. **§ 741.24(2),** and the school's recovery from the minors' parents will be offset against any amounts the school recovers as treble damages, pursuant to **Florida Statutes section 812.035(7) (2006).**

☞ Same section and subsection; use id.
☞ Same section, new subsection; use id. plus new subsection number.

☞ First cite to new chapter [812] and section [035]: use full citation. This is an embedded citation; spell out "section."

4 Constitutions

Bluebook Rules 11 and B7 control the form for citations to the Federal and state constitutions.

- **Basic Rule:** Federal or state constitutions are cited by including:

    (1) **The name of the jurisdiction.**
    - *Citation Sentences and Clauses:* Abbreviate according to Table 10.
    - *Textual Sentences:* Spell out the name of the jurisdiction.

    (2) **The word Constitution.**
    - *Citation Sentences and Clauses:* Abbreviate to "Const."
    - *Textual Sentences:* Spell out the word "Constitution."

    (3) **The word article or amendment (as appropriate),** follow by a comma.
    - *Citation Sentences and Clauses:* Abbreviate to "art." or "amend" according to Table 16.
    - *Textual Sentences:* Spell out the words "article" or "amendment."

    (4) **The article or amendment number,** expressed in <u>roman</u> numerals.

    (5) **A section symbol or the word "section."**
    - *Citation Sentences and Clauses*: Use the section symbol [§].
    - *Textual Sentences:* Spell out the word "section."

    (6) **The number of the section being cited,** in <u>arabic</u> numerals.

(1)   (2)   (3) (4) (5)(6)
U.S. Const. art. III, § 3.

(1)		(2)		(3)		(4)	(5)		(6)
Jurisdiction	+	Const.	+	art. or amend. & No.	+	§	+		No.

- **Basic Rule: Pinpoints.** To pinpoint a particular clause of a constitution:

    (1) **Citation sentences and clauses:** Add the abbreviation "cl." followed by the clause number. Use arabic numerals.

    (2) **Textual sentences:** Spell out the word clause followed by the clause number. Use arabic numerals.

- **Basic Rule: Short Forms.** Use only <u>id.</u> If <u>id.</u> cannot be used because other citation intervene, use a full citation.

- **Basic Rule: Common Names or Short Titles.** In textual sentences, once a full citation has been given you may refer to an article, amendment, or clause by a common name, or a shortened version of the name.

Examples: Constitutions

	TEXTUAL SENTENCES	**CITATION SENTENCES & CLAUSES**
Article	United States Constitution article II	U.S. Const. art. II.
	Pennsylvania Constitution article XII	Pa. Const. art. XII.
Section	United States Constitution article II, section 1	U.S. Const. art. II, § 1.
	Pennsylvania Constitution article I, section 9	Pa. Const. art. I, § 9.
Clause	United States Constitution article II, section 1, clause 7	U.S. Const. art. II, § 1, cl. 7.
	California Constitution article IX, section 9, clause (d)	Cal. Const. art. IX ,§ 9, cl. (d).
Amendment	United States Constitution amendment V	U.S. Const. amend. V.
	Arkansas Constitution amendment 80, § 16	Ark. Const. amend. 80, § 16.
Short Form	Article II requires	<u>Id.</u>
	The Fifth Amendment provides	

Important Note

The preceding discussion covers basic citation rules only. *The Bluebook* **has special rules for citations to repealed constitutional provisions, provisions that have been subsequently amended, or constitutions that have been superseded. See** *Bluebook* **Rule 11 if you encounter any of these situations.**

5 Secondary Sources

Bluebook **Rules 15-19 and B8-9** control the form for citations to secondary sources. This chapter discusses citations to the following sources:

A. Treatises and books;

B. Periodicals;

C. Legal encyclopedias;

D. Legal dictionaries;

E. American Law Reports (A.L.R.) annotations; and

F. Restatements.

A. Treatises and Books   Rule 15

- **Basic Rule:** Provide the following information, <u>in ordinary roman type</u>:

    (1) Author's full name, followed by a comma;

    (2) Book title, underlined (or italicized ♦);

    (3) Pinpoint page(s) or section(s);

    (4) If applicable, publication information, including edition; and

    (5) Year of publication.

(1)	(2)	(3)	(4)	(5)
Author's full name +	**Book Title** +	**Pinpoint Page or Section** +	**Publication Info.** +	**Year**

        (1)   (2)   (3) (4)   (5)

Lawrence M. Friedman, <u>A History of American Law</u> 192 (3d ed. 2005).

☞ Pay careful attention to comma placement. Place a comma after the author's name, but not between the book title and the page number.

(1) Author's Full Name   Rule 15.1

- **Basic Rule: Single Author.** Provide the full name of the author, given name first, and including any designations such as Jr., Sr., etc.

- **Basic Rule: Multiple Authors.** Provide the full names of all authors, given name first, and including any designations such as Jr., Sr., etc., subject to the limitations below.

  - **Two authors:** Provide both names, separated by an ampersand [&].

  - **More than two authors:** You may either:

    (a) Provide the first-listed author only, followed by the words "et al." (preferred method); **OR**
    (b) List all authors' names, separated by commas, using an ampersand [&] before the last author's name.

      ☞ If the book or treatise has more than three authors, use method (a) unless there is a compelling reason to list all authors.

Examples: Authors

Single Author	**Wayne R. LaFave**, <u>Criminal Law</u> 293 (4th ed. 2003).
Two Authors	**Jeff Koon & Andy Powell**, <u>You May Not Tie an Alligator to a Fire Hydrant: 101 Real Dumb Laws</u> 15 (2d. ed. 2002).
Multiple Authors	**Robert M. Jarvis et al.**, <u>Bush v. Gore: The Fight for Florida's Vote</u> 63-64 (2001). **or** **Robert M. Jarvis, Phyllis Coleman & Johnny C. Burris**, <u>Bush v. Gore: The Fight for Florida's Vote</u> 63-64 (2001).

(2) Book Title   Rule 15.3

- **Basic Rule:** Provide the full title of the book, omitting subtitles unless particularly relevant. Underline (or italicize ♦) the title. Do not abbreviate any words in the title. Capitalize the first letter of each word except articles, conjunctions, and prepositions, unless they begin the title's name.

articles	☞	a, an, the
conjunctions	☞	and, or, but, etc.
prepositions	☞	to, for, in, etc.

☞ **See examples of book titles in the chart above.**

(3) Pinpoint Page or Section   Rule 3

- **Basic Rule:** Always provide the exact page or section you are referring to, subject to the following rules.

  - **Multiple Pages:** To cite more than one page, follow *Bluebook* Rule 3.2. See page 39 of this guide for additional information on citing multiple pages.

  - **Sections:** If the work is divided into sections, cite to the individual section number, not the page number. To cite multiple sections, follow *Bluebook* Rule 3.3(b). See page 59 of this guide for additional information on citing multiple sections.

  - **Volumes:** If the work consists of more than one volume, place the volume number *before* the author's name.

Examples: Pinpoint Page or Section

Multiple pages	Michael P. Scharf, <u>Balkan Justice</u> **51-53** (1997).
Sections	Thomas A. Dickerson, <u>Travel Law</u> **§ 2.07** (2005).
Volumes	**7** Marilyn Mizner et al., <u>Damages in Tort Actions</u> 112-13 (1982).

(4) Publication Information   Rule 15.4

- **Basic Rule:** Include any applicable publication information in parentheses at the end of the citation, as follows:

  - **Editions:** If the book has **more than one edition**, include the edition number in the date parentheses. Cite to the edition you are using (generally this will be the latest edition). If the book has only **one edition**, omit the edition information.

  - **Supplements:** To cite information in a book supplement, include "Supp." in the parentheses, following *Bluebook* Rule 3.1(c).

Examples: Publication Information

Single edition	Jeffrey M. Gaba, <u>Environmental Law</u> 211 (2005).
Multiple editions	Lawrence Taylor, <u>Drunk Driving Defense</u> 15 (**5th ed.** 2000).
Supplements	Burns H. Weston et al., <u>International Law and World Order</u> 17 (**Supp.** 2004).

(5) Year

- **Basic Rule:** Include the year of publication in parentheses at the end of the citation; this will generally be the copyright year.

Short Forms: Treatises & Books   Rules 15.9, 4, & B8.2

- **Basic Rule:** Once a full citation has been given for a book or treatise, a short form may be used, following the rules below.

  1. <u>Id.:</u> If there has been no intervening cite to different authority, use <u>id.</u>, either alone or combined with a new pinpoint page number. See discussion of <u>id.</u> on pages 34–35 of this guide for general information on using <u>id.</u>

  2. <u>Supra</u>: If there has been an intervening citation to different authority, use <u>supra</u>. A <u>supra</u> cite consists of:

     (1) Author's last name, followed by a comma;

     (2) The word "supra" which is underlined (or italicized ♦), followed by a comma;

     (3) The word "at," if citing a page; and

     (4) A pinpoint page or section number.

Examples: Short Form Citation for Treatises & Books

No intervening cite, same page or section	<u>Id.</u>
No intervening cite, new page or section	<u>Id.</u> at 135. <u>Id.</u> § 14.
After intervening cite to different authority	Koon & Powell, <u>supra</u>, at 17. Dickerson, <u>supra</u>, § 4.01(4).

Important Note

The preceding discussion covers basic citation rules only. *The Bluebook* has special rules for citations to works in a collection, collected documents, and serials. Special rules apply to institutional authors, editors and translators, and citations to prefaces, forewords, introductions and epilogues. See *Bluebook* Rule 15 if you encounter any of these situations.

B. Periodicals (Law Reviews & Journals)   Rules 16 & B9

- **Basic Rule:** Provide the following information, <u>in ordinary roman type</u>:

  (1) Author's full name, followed by a comma;

  (2) Article title, underlined (or italicized ♦), followed by a comma;

  (3) Volume number, if available;

  (4) Name of periodical, abbreviated according to *Bluebook* Table 13;

  (5) Beginning page number;

  (6) Pinpoint page(s); and

  (7) Publication year.

(1)	(2)	(3)	(4)	(5)	(6)	(7)
Author	Title	Volume No.	Periodical Name	Beginning Page	Pinpoint Page	Year

(1)   (2)   (3) (4)   (5) (6) (7)
Shaun P. Martin, <u>The Radical Necessity Defense</u>, 73 U. Cin. L. Rev. 1527, 1549 (2005).

(1) Author's Full Name   Rule 16.1

- **Basic Rule:** Provide the full name of the author(s), given name first. Include designations such as Jr., Sr., etc.

  ☞ Follow the same rules for authors as for treatises and books on page 68 of this guide, including rules for multiple authors.

☞ Occasionally a student-written work is not "signed," i.e., it does not include the author's name. To cite an unsigned work, omit the author's name but provide the rest of the citation information.

  ☞ In some student-written works, the author's name appears at the *end* of the piece. Always check thoroughly before concluding the work is "unsigned."

(2) Article Title   Rule 16.2

- **Basic Rule: Articles.** Provide the full title of the article, underlined (or italicized ♦). Capitalize the first letter of each word except articles, conjunctions, or prepositions, unless it is the first word in the title. **Do not abbreviate** words in the article title.

- **Basic Rule: Comments, Notes and Recent Developments (Student-Written Works).** Cite the same manner as other works, but include the designation of the piece (Comment, Note, Recent Development, etc.) after the author's name, separated by a comma.

  ☞ Refer to the special rules found in *Bluebook* Rule 16.6.2 when citing to student-written works, and the examples in this section of the guide.

(3) Volume   Rule 16.3

- **Basic Rule:** Provide the volume number, if available.

  ☞ Occasionally there will be no volume number, in which case you would omit it. Sometimes the volume number will be expressed as a year, which is treated as a volume number.

(4) Periodical Name   Rule 16.3

- **Basic Rule:** Provide the abbreviated name of the periodical, using the abbreviations found in *Bluebook* Table 13.

  ☞ Occasionally an abbreviation for the periodical you are citing will not be found in Table 13. If this occurs, use Table 13 as a guide to create an appropriate abbreviation. For example, "Law Journal" is always abbreviated "L.J."

(5) Beginning Page   Rule 16.3

- **Basic Rule:** Provide the page number where the article begins.

(6) Pinpoint Page(s)   Rule 16.3

- **Basic Rule:** Always provide the exact pinpoint page you are referring to. Follow the same pinpoint citation rules used for cases, including the rules for citing to multiple pages. See pages 31 and 39 of this guide for additional information.

(7) Year   Rule 16.3

- **Basic Rule:** Include in parentheses the year of publication, generally the copyright year.

Examples: Periodicals

Single Author	**Jay Dratler, Jr.**, Alice in Wonderland Meets the U.S. Patent System, 38 Akron L. Rev. 299, 320 (2005).
Multiple Authors	**Noel B. Cunningham & James R. Repetti**, Textualism and Tax Shelters, 24 Va. Tax Rev. 1, 47 (2004).
Comment	Pamela M. Keeney, **Comment**, Frozen Assets of Terrorists and Terrorist Supporters: A Proposed Solution to the Creditor Collection Problem, 21 Bankr. Dev. J. 301, 328 (2004).
Note	Robin Andrews, **Note**, Copyright Infringement and the Internet: An Economic Analysis of Crime, 11 B.U. J. Sci. & Tech. L. 256, 262 (2005).
Recent Development	Sumayyah Waheed, **Recent Development**, Domestic Violence on the Reservation: Imperfect Laws, Imperfect Solution, 19 Berkeley Women's L.J. 287, 298 (2004).

Short Forms: Periodicals   Rules 16.7 & B9.2

- **Basic Rule:** After giving a citation in full, use either id. or supra on subsequent references. See pages 34 (id.) and 70 (supra) of this guide for further information about these short forms.

Important Note

The preceding discussion covers basic citation rules for law reviews and journals, the most frequently cited periodicals. *The Bluebook* has special rules for citations to magazines (Rule 16.4), newspapers (Rule 16.5), institutional publications (Rule 16.6.7), and other types of periodicals. See *Bluebook* Rules 16 if you encounter any of these situations.

C. Legal Encyclopedias   Rule 15.8

- **Basic Rule:** Provide the following information, in <u>ordinary roman type</u>:

  (1) Volume number;

  (2) Name of encyclopedia, abbreviated as shown in Rule 15.8;

  (3) Title of article or entry, underlined (or italicized ◆);

  (4) Section symbol [§];

  (5) Section number; and

  (6) Year of publication.

(1)		(2)		(3)		(4)		(5)		(6)
Vol. No.	+	**Abbreviated Name of Encyclopedia**	+	**Article Title**	+	**§**	+	**Section No.**	+	**Year**

(1)   (2)   (3)   (4)(5)   (6)
7 Am. Jur. 2d <u>Attorneys at Law</u> § 68 (2004).

Examples: Encyclopedias

ENCYCLOPEDIA	COVERAGE	EXAMPLE OF CITATION
American Jurisprudence	National	16A Am. Jur. <u>Constitutional Law</u> § 369 (2004).
Corpus Juris Secundum	National	60 C.J.S. <u>Motor Vehicles</u> §§ 50, 52 (2002). [Citing multiple sections; notice two § symbols.]
State Encyclopedias Follow the general form for citations to state encyclopedias, changing the encyclopedia name as needed. Use Table 10 for abbreviations.	Florida Ohio New York	7 Fla. Jur. <u>Boats, Ships, and Shipping</u> § 53 (2004). 1 Ohio Jur. <u>Abandoned, Lost, and Escheated Property</u> § 2 (2003). 2 N.Y. Jur. <u>Administrative Law</u> § 118 (2003).

Short Forms: Encyclopedias   Rule 15.9

- **Basic Rule:** After giving a citation in full, use either <u>id.</u> or <u>supra</u> on subsequent references. See pages 34 (<u>id.</u>) and 70 (<u>supra</u>) of this guide for additional help with these short forms. Substitute the article's title for the author's name when using <u>supra</u>. <u>See</u> *Bluebook* Rule 4.2.

D. Legal Dictionaries   Rules 15.8 & B8.1

- **Basic Rule:** Provide the following information in <u>ordinary roman type</u>:

    (1) Dictionary name, underlined or italicized ♦;

    (2) Pinpoint page number;

    (3) Edition number; and

    (4) Year of publication.

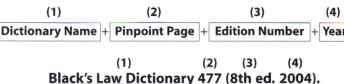

Short Forms: Dictionaries   Rule 15.9

- **Basic Rule:** After giving a citation in full, use either <u>id.</u> or <u>supra</u> on subsequent references. See pages 34 (<u>id.</u>) and 70 (<u>supra</u>) of this guide for additional help with these short forms. Use the name of the dictionary in place of the author's name in a <u>supra</u> citation, following *Bluebook* Rule 4.2.

E. American Law Reports (A.L.R.) Annotations　　　Rule 16.6.6

- **Basic Rule:** Provide the following information, <u>in ordinary roman type</u>:

  (1) Author (if available, otherwise omit), followed by a comma;

  (2) The word "Annotation," followed by a comma;

  (3) Title of annotation, underlined (or italicized ♦), followed by a comma;

  (4) Volume number;

  (5) Abbreviation for American Law Reports ["A.L.R."], followed by the series number [3d, 4th, 5th, 6th, Fed. or Fed. 2d];

  (6) Beginning page number;

  (7) Pinpoint page number; and

  (8) Year of publication.

(1)	(2)	(3)	(4)	(5)	(6)	(7)	(8)
Author	+ "Annotation"	+ Title	+ Vol.	+ A.L.R. & Series	+ Beginning Page	+ Pinpoint	+ Year

　　　　(1)　　　　　　　(2)　　　　　　　　　　　　　(3)　　　　　　　　　　(4)　　(5)　　(6)
George L. Blum, Annotation, <u>Religion as a Factor in Child Custody Cases</u>, 124 A.L.R.5th 203,

　(7)　(8)
212 (2004).

Examples: Annotations

A.L.R. Federal Series	Jason Binimow, Annotation, <u>Designation as Unlawful or Enemy Combatant</u>, 185 A.L.R. Fed. 475, 490 (2003).
A.L.R. 5th Series	Randy J. Sutton, Annotation, <u>Products Liability: Paints, Stains, and Similar Products</u>, 69 A.L.R.5th 131, 139 (1999).

Note: In the federal series example there is one space between A.L.R. and Fed., but there are no spaces in "A.L.R.5th." See the spacing rules on page 16 of this guide.

Short Forms: A.L.R.s　　　　　　　　　　　　　Rule 16.7

- **Basic Rule:** After giving a citation in full, use either <u>id.</u> or <u>supra</u> on subsequent references. See pages 34 (<u>id.</u>) and 70 (<u>supra</u>) of this guide for additional help with short forms.

F. Restatements   Rules 12.8.5 & B6.1.3

- **Basic Rule:** Always provide the following information <u>in ordinary roman type</u>. Abbreviate any words found in *Bluebook* Table 6.

  (1) The word "Restatement";

  (2) Series number (if applicable) placed in parentheses;

  (3) The word "of";

  (4) Subject (e.g., Torts, Contracts, etc.), abbreviated as appears in Table 6;

  (5) Section symbol [§];

  (6) Section number; and

  (7) Year of Publication.

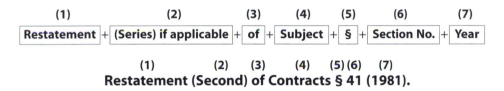

(1)   (2)   (3)   (4) (5)(6)   (7)
Restatement (Second) of Contracts § 41 (1981).

- **Basic Rule: Sections.** For Restatements that are not further divided into subtitles, cite to the section. See example below.

- **Basic Rule: Subtitles.** For Restatements that have subtitles dividing larger sections, include the subtitle following the subject. A colon follows the subject title. See example below.

- **Basic Rule: Comments.** To cite to a comment to a Restatement section, insert the abbreviation "cmt." followed by the comment number or letter, after the section number. See example below.

- **Basic Rule: Illustrations.** To cite an illustration of a Restatement rule, include the comment number or letter, followed by the abbreviation "illus." and the illustration number. See example below.

Examples: Restatements

Section	Restatement (Second) of Judgments **§ 49** (1988)
Subtitle	Restatement (Third) of Torts: **Liab. for Physical Harms** § 14 (2005).
Comment	Restatement (Third) of Torts: Liab. for Physical Harms § 14 **cmt. c** (2005).
Illustration	Restatement (Third) of the Law Governing Lawyers § 96 **cmt. e, illus. 1** (2000).

Short Forms: Restatements   Rule 4

- **Basic Rule:** After giving a citation in full, use **only** id. on subsequent references. If id. cannot be used because of an intervening citation to other authority, use a full citation. DO NOT use supra (see *Bluebook* Rule 4.2). See page 34 of this guide for additional help with id. short forms.

Important Note

The preceding discussion covers basic citation rules for the most frequently cited secondary sources. *The Bluebook* has special rules for citations to other secondary sources. Check the index in *The Bluebook* for citation rules to sources not governed by this guide.

6 Procedural and Court Rules

Bluebook Rule 12.8.3 controls the form for citations to procedural and court rules. This chapter discusses citations to the following:

A. Federal rules of procedure and evidence; and

B. Local court rules.

All courts, whether federal or state, have rules regulating the conduct of business before the court. These rules range from federal rules of procedure and evidence governing litigation in all federal courts, to local rules applicable to how business is conducted in a particular courthouse. *The Bluebook* provides general guidance for citing procedural and court rules, but many jurisdictions provide their own citation forms. If local rules provide a citation form, use that form instead of *Bluebook* form, as discussed in Part B., below.

A. Federal Rules of Procedure & Evidence   Rule 12.8.3

- **Basic Rule:** Provide the following information, in <u>ordinary roman type</u>:

  (1) The abbreviation "Fed. R." indicating citation to a federal rule;

  (2) The particular type of rule cited (civil procedure, evidence, etc.), abbreviated following the examples in Rule 12.8.3; and

  (3) The specific rule number being cited.

(1)		(2)		(3)
"Fed. R."	+	Type of Rule	+	Rule Number

(1)   (2) (3)
Fed. R. Civ. P. 59

Examples: Federal Rules

Rules of Civil Procedure	Fed. R. Civ. P. 12.
Rules of Criminal Procedure	Fed. R. Crim. P. 28.
Rules of Evidence	Fed. R. Evid. 802.
Rules of Appellate Procedure	Fed. R. App. P. 21.

B. Local Rules: State & Federal Courts   Rule 12.8.3

- **Basic Rule:** To cite a rule of court, follow these steps <u>in order</u>:

  1. Check the court's website for a specific rule regarding citation to that court's rules (see below). If the court has a specific citation rule, follow it.

  2. If there is no specific citation rule on the website (or if the rule states to follow *Bluebook* citation rules), check *Bluebook* Rule 12.8.3 for the general way court rules are cited.

  3. Assemble the citation following the court's specific rules or, if following *Bluebook* rules, by providing the information diagramed below, using <u>ordinary roman type</u>. Explanations for each part of the citation follow.

(1)		(2)		(3)
Court Issuing Rule	+	Abbreviation indicating "Court Rule"	+	Rule Number

(1)   (2)   (3)
N.J. R. 1:1-3

How to Find Local Rules

Many courts include citation forms in their local rules. The best source for citing information is the court's own website. To locate a court's website, check these places:

1. *Bluebook* Table 1 entries include the main court website for each jurisdiction. The main website will usually provide links to individual courts in the jurisdiction.

2. LLRX.com, a free site, maintains a comprehensive collection of links to court rules on court websites, available at: http://www.llrx.com/courtrules/.

Once you have found the court's website:

- (a) Check Bluepages Table BT.2, which provides "cite as" entries for some courts. The entry will provide the rule number(s) to look up on the court's website.

- (b) If the specific court's "cite as" rule is not listed in Table BT.2, look in the rules index on the court's website (most courts index their rules).

- (c) If you cannot find a "cite as" rule listed in the rules index, look for other likely spots. If the court has specific citation rules, they will usually be found in the first few rules, perhaps labeled as introductory, prefatory, or miscellaneous rules.

(1) Court Issuing Rule – *Bluebook* Form

- **Basic Rule:** Provide the abbreviated name of the court issuing the Rule, using the following for guidance:

  (a) *Bluebook* **Rule 12.8.3**, for general guidance on citation to court rules.

  (b) *Bluebook* **Table 10**, for geographical term abbreviations.

  ☞ For state courts, include the abbreviated name of the state.

  ☞ For federal district courts, include the name of the state, and any subdivision within that state:

  Example: Southern District Ohio   ☞   S.D. Ohio

  (c) *Bluebook* **Table 7**, lists abbreviations for court names. If the rules apply to a particular division of the jurisdiction's courts (e.g., circuit, district, appeals), or if the court handles only special types of matters (e.g., probate or family courts), include that designation.

  Examples:

  Fourth District   ☞   4th Dist. Ct.

  State courts only; district is abbreviated "D." in federal courts. <u>See</u> Table 7.

  Probate Court   ☞   Prob. Ct.

  Family Court   ☞   Fam. Ct.

(2) Abbreviation for Court Rule – *Bluebook* Form

- **Basic Rule:** Provide an abbreviation to identify the cite as a court rule as opposed to another type of authority. In the following examples, spacing has been marked with a •; see spacing rules on page 16 of this guide.

  Examples:

  Court Rule   ☞   Ct.•R.

  Local Rule   ☞   L.R.

  Civil Procedure Rule   ☞   Civ.•P.

  Criminal Procedure Rule   ☞   Crim.•P.

(3) Rule Number – *Bluebook* Form

- **Basic Rule:** Provide the rule number for the specific rule you are citing, in the format used by the local rules themselves, or by example from *Bluebook* Rule 12.8.3.

Examples: Court Rules

JURISDICTION	EXAMPLE OF CITATION FORM
United States Supreme Court 　*Bluebook* **form**	Sup. Ct. R. 24.
United States 11th Circuit Court of Appeals 　**Local rule specifies *Bluebook* form**	11th Cir. R. 15-4.
United State District Court of Idaho 　**Local rule specifies citation form**	Dist. Idaho Loc. Crim. R. 46.1.
Kansas Supreme Court 　**No local rules specify form; use** 　***Bluebook* form**	Kan. Sup. Ct. R. 105.
Kansas Johnson County Juvenile Court 　**No local rules specify form; use *Bluebook* form**	Johnson County Juv. R. 4.

☞ **Don't forget to check the Court's website and conform your rule to any specific requirements.**

☞ **See additional examples of court rule citations in *Bluebook* Rule 12.8.3.**

Short Forms: Court Rules   Rule 4

- **Basic Rule:** After giving a citation in full, use **only** <u>id.</u> on subsequent references. If <u>id.</u> cannot be used because of an intervening citation to other authority, use a full citation. DO NOT use <u>supra</u> (<u>see</u> *Bluebook* Rule 4.2). See page 34 of this guide for additional help with <u>id.</u> short forms.

7 Litigation Documents and Record Citations

Bluebook **Rule B10** controls the form for citations to documents filed in trial courts (litigation documents) and citations to the record in appellate court cases.

In documents submitted to trial courts, it may be necessary to refer to other documents previously submitted that are a part of the court file for the litigation. These are generally referred to as "litigation documents" and may include motions, deposition transcripts, complaints or answers, to name just a few. If a case is in the appellate stage, an official record of the proceedings in the lower court is created called the "record on appeal," or simply the "record." Consult *Bluebook* Rule B10 for guidance on citation forms for litigation documents and the record.

- **Basic Rule:** To cite a litigation document or the record, provide the following information, **in parentheses**, using <u>ordinary roman type</u>:

  (1) Title of document, abbreviated if appropriate;

  (2) Pinpoint citation to the exact page, paragraph, or section of the document;

  (3) Date, if necessary to distinguish between multiple documents of the same title.

(1)   (2)   (3)

(**Abbreviated Title of Document** + **Pinpoint Citation** + **Date, if necessary**)

(1)   (2)
(Def.'s Mot. Summ. J. 14.)

(1)   (2)   (3)
(Snyder Aff. ¶ 22, Jan. 16, 2007.)

(1)   (2)
(R. at 215-17.)

- **Basic Rule: Punctuation.** Place punctuation (periods) inside or outside of the citation parentheses according to the following rules:

  (a) **Citation Sentences:** Include the period INSIDE the closing parenthesis when the citation appears in a citation sentence.

  (b) **Citation Clauses:** Place the period OUTSIDE the closing parenthesis if the citation appears as a citation clause at the <u>end</u> of a textual sentence. If the citation appears in the middle of a textual sentence, do not punctuate. DO NOT set off the citation clause with commas.

Examples: Punctuation in Litigation Documents

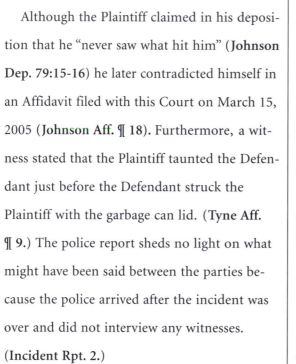

> Although the Plaintiff claimed in his deposition that he "never saw what hit him" (**Johnson Dep. 79:15-16**) he later contradicted himself in an Affidavit filed with this Court on March 15, 2005 (**Johnson Aff. ¶ 18**). Furthermore, a witness stated that the Plaintiff taunted the Defendant just before the Defendant struck the Plaintiff with the garbage can lid. (**Tyne Aff. ¶ 9.**) The police report sheds no light on what might have been said between the parties because the police arrived after the incident was over and did not interview any witnesses. (**Incident Rpt. 2.**)

☞ **Punctuation Rule (b):** Citation clause; no punctuation.

☞ **Punctuation Rule (b):** Citation clause; no punctuation in citation, but include sentence-ending punctuation following closing parenthesis.

☞ **Punctuation Rule (a):** Citation sentence; period placed inside parentheses.

☞ **Punctuation Rule (a):** Citation sentence; period placed inside parentheses.

(1) Abbreviated Title of Document   Rule B10.1

- **Basic Rule: Citation Sentences and Clauses.** Provide the title of the document, abbreviated according to Table BT.1.

  ☞ Abbreviate <u>only</u> in citations. If the title of the document is embedded as part of a textual sentence, do not abbreviate.

Examples: Abbreviated Document Titles

Citation Sentence Abbreviate title of document in citations only.	The Defendant's motion cites the <u>Smith</u> case to make a similar point. (**Def.'s Mot. Summ. J.** 12:16-17.)
Textual Sentence & Citation Sentence Do not abbreviate title embedded in a textual sentence; abbreviate title of document in citation sentence.	The **Motion for Summary Judgment** cites the <u>Smith</u> case to make to make a similar point. (**Def.'s Mot. Summ. J.** 12:16-17.)

- **Basic Rule: Record Citations.** To cite to the "Record," abbreviate to "R."

    Example: To cite page 15 of the Record   ☞   (R. at 15.)

- **Basic Rule: Abbreviations Not Found in BT.1.** If the document is not listed in Table BT.1, create an abbreviation, but ONLY if it the reference will be unambiguous. When in doubt, spell it out.

    ☞ For example, neither "incident" nor "report" appear in Table BT.1. In a citation to an Incident Report, it would be difficult to abbreviate the word "incident" in a way that would not be confusing. Inc.? Inci.? Incid.? Rather than risk confusion, spell it out. However, "report" is widely abbreviated as Rpt. and adopting that abbreviation is unlikely to cause confusion in this context.

- **Basic Rule: Multiple Documents with Same Title.** If more than one document with the same title appears in the litigation file (e.g., multiple depositions, affidavits, or similar), provide the name of the person who gave the deposition or affidavit, or use some other term that distinguishes the document from other similar documents in the litigation. Dates may also be used to distinguish litigation documents (see section (3) below).

Examples: Multiple Documents with Same Title

Instead of	☞	*Do This*
(Dep. 37.)	☞	(Hardy Dep. 37.)
(Aff. ¶ 13.)	☞	(Tarper Aff. ¶ 13.)
(Mot. Summ. J. 6.)	☞	(Def.'s Mot. Summ. J. 6.)

(2) Pinpoint Citations   Rule B10.3

- **Basic Rule:** For any document exceeding one page in length, give a pinpoint cite to the page on which the cited material appears. If the document is subdivided into numbered paragraphs or lines, always pinpoint the exact subdivision being cited, according to the following rules:

  (a) **Page numbers in litigation documents:** Provide the page number(s) after the document title. In <u>litigation documents</u>, DO NOT use "at" to separate the title and page number. For cites to the <u>record</u>, see (d), below.

  (b) **Paragraph numbers:** Include a paragraph symbol [¶] followed by a space and the paragraph number. If citing more than one paragraph, include two paragraph symbols [¶¶], following *Bluebook* Rule 3.3(c).

  (c) **Line numbers:** Provide the page number on which the lines appear, followed by a colon and the specific line numbers. There are no spaces between the page number, colon, and line numbers.

  (d) **Record citations:** Provide the page number(s), preceded by the word "at." This rule does not apply to litigation documents.

Examples: Pinpoint Citations

Rule (a)	Plaintiff's Reply Brief, page 3	☞	(Pl.'s Reply Br. **3**.)
Rule (b)	Southern Affidavit, paragraph 29.	☞	(Southern Aff. **¶ 29**.)
	Northern Affidavit, paragraphs 26 and 27.		(Northern Aff. **¶¶ 26-27**.)
Rule (c)	Taft Deposition, page 86, lines 18 through 22	☞	(Taft Dep. **86:18-22**.)
	Taft Deposition, page 97, line 23, through page 98, line 4.		(Taft Dep. **97:23-98:4**.)
Rule (d)	Appellate Record, page 1102.	☞	(R. **at** 1102.)
See additional examples in Rule B10.3.			

(3) Date
Rule B10.4

- **Basic Rule: Litigation Documents Only.** If multiple documents of the same title appear in the litigation file, and they cannot be adequately distinguished by including a reference to a party or person involved in the litigation, provide the date of the document to differentiate it from similar documents. Separate the date from the main portion of the citation by a comma.

Examples: Multiple Documents with Same Title

If This Occurs	☞	Then Do This
To cite one of the five Verified Statements that witness Jack Jones gave after an automobile accident.	☞	(Jones V.S. ¶ 12, **Oct. 2, 2004.**)
To cite one specific letter (of many) sent by Defendant to Plaintiff.	☞	(Def.'s. Ltr. to Pl., **Dec. 11, 2003.**) Note: Although the abbreviation for letter does not appear in Table BT.1, it is a commonly used abbreviation and unlikely to lead to confusion in this context.

Short Forms: Litigation & Record Citations
Rule B10.5

- **Basic Rule:** On subsequent references, use a short form that will clearly convey to the reader which document is being cited. <u>Id.</u> may be used, if appropriate, or a shortened version of the full citation. See examples in Rule B10.5.

- ◆ Some practitioners prefer that the <u>id.</u> short form not be used when citing to the Appellate Record (inasmuch as the citation itself is often shorter than the short form). Ask your professor or supervisor which form is preferred.

8 Signals and Explanatory Parentheticals

Bluebook **Rules 1.2-1.5** in the White Pages and Bluepages **Rules B4 and B11** control the form for signals and parentheticals. These tools are used to concisely convey information about a case without providing a detailed discussion. This chapter discusses the following:

A. Signals;

B. Explanatory parentheticals; and

C. Combining multiple signals and parentheticals, and string citing multiple authorities.

A. Signals   Rules 1.2 & B4

An introductory signal is a word or term telling the reader the type of support the cited authority provides for the accompanying text. A signal provides a shorthand context for the citation. *The Bluebook* authorizes eleven signals, divided into four categories of relationship support:

(a) **Signals Indicating SUPPORT**	(b) **Signal Indicating COMPARISON**	(c) **Signals Indicating CONTRADICTION**	(d) **Signal indicating BACKGROUND**
No signal E.g. Accord See See also Cf.	Compare	Contra But see But c.f.	See generally

- **Basic Rule:** Signals precede the cited authority, and must be underlined [or italicized ♦]. Capitalize the signal only if it begins a <u>citation sentence</u>.

  ☞ Note: There is a break in the underlining between the signal and the beginning of the case name (represented in the example below by a •).

<u>See</u> • <u>Stone v. State</u>, 74 S.W.3d 591, 594 (Ark. 2001).

☞ *Bluebook* Rule 1.2. explains the purpose of each signal, and the information each conveys. Pay careful attention to *The Bluebook*'s description of the proper use of a signal; a misused signal may convey a message that is the opposite of the one you intended.

Examples: Signals

This chart briefly explains and shows examples of the more commonly used signals. There are additional signals (see above) which are explained in *Bluebook* Rule 1.2.		
Signal	**Explanation**	**Example**
No Signal	Cited authority directly states the proposition. ☞ The absence of a signal is the most commonly used signal.	A warrantless entry into a private residence is presumptively unreasonable under the Fourth Amendment. <u>Love v. State</u>, 355 Ark. 334, 341 (2003).
E.g.,	Cited authority directly states the proposition, but it is not helpful to discuss it in detail. ☞ Note that the <u>e.g.</u> signal is the only signal followed by a comma.	The court has made it abundantly clear that it can affirm a decision by the trial court, albeit for a different reason. <u>McCoy v. State</u>, 347 Ark. 913, 924 (2002); **e.g.,** <u>Williams v. State</u>, 343 Ark. 591, 604 (2001).
Accord	More than one authority states the proposition but the text refers to only one. ☞ Often used to show the law of one jurisdiction is in accord with the law of another.	The ADEA provides for an award of liquidated damages when the employer "knew or showed reckless disregard whether its conduct was prohibited by the statute." <u>Hazen Paper Co. v. Biggins</u>, 507 U.S. 604, 617 (1993); **accord**, <u>Trans World Airlines, Inc. v. Thurston</u>, 469 U.S. 111, 126 (1985).
See	Cited authority does not directly state the proposition, but obviously follows from it. ☞ This signal requires the reader to take an inferential step.	That presumption may be overcome, however, if the police officer obtained consent to conduct a warrantless search. **See** <u>Stone v. State</u>, 348 Ark. 661, 669 (2001).
See also	Cited authority supports the proposition, but will not be discussed. ☞ Use a parenthetical to explain why the case is relevant.	**See also** Ark. R. Crim. P. 11.1 (2003) ("An officer may conduct searches and make seizures without a search warrant or other color of authority if consent is given to the search or seizure.").

Examples: Signals *continued*

Signal	Explanation	Example
But see	Cited authority clearly supports a proposition contrary to the stated proposition. ☞ While it is not necessary to provide a parenthetical explaining the contradictory authority, it usually is best to include some explanation.	This circuit generally uses the terms "adverse employment action" and "tangible employment action" interchangeably. Phelan v. Cook County, 463 F.3d 773, 785 (7th Cir. 2006). **But see** Lutkewitte v. Gonzales, 436 F.3d 248, 262 (D.C. Cir. 2006) (discussing conflict among circuits as to whether terms are interchangeable).
See generally	Cited authority gives background information that may be helpful but will not be discussed.	Dismissal is appropriate when the defendants fail to raise a triable issue of fact in opposition. **See generally** Granillo v. Donna Karen Co., 793 N.Y.S.2d 465 (2005).

B. Explanatory Parentheticals   Rules 1.5 & B11

An explanatory parenthetical provides information about an authority (typically a case) without the need for a detailed discussion in the text. Parentheticals can be used to provide context for an authority, or to clarify the reason for the citation.

- **Basic Rule:** Explain in parentheses at the end of the citation the relevance of the proposition cited, or provide additional information to put the authority in context. Parenthetical information should be as concise as possible without sacrificing clarity.

  ☞ Explanatory phrases often begin with the **present participle** form of a verb (one that ends with *-ing*). However, if the context of the citation makes a participial phrase unnecessary, a shorter phrase may be used.

Examples: Explanatory Parentheticals

With Participial Phrase [Holding, explaining, finding, quoting, citing, interpreting, etc.]	Various items may be considered dangerous weapons, but rope is not one of them. <u>Smith v. Baldwin</u>, 466 F.3d 805, 818 (9th Cir. 2006) (**finding** no evidence suggesting that the rope qualified as a dangerous weapon under Or. Rev. Stat. § 161.015(1)-(2) (2003)).
	An outcry by a victim is a circumstance which the jury can consider on the question of corroboration. <u>Riggins v. State</u>, 226 Ga. 381, 385 (Ga. 1970) (**rejecting** defendant's argument that an outcry goes only to the question of consent and not to the corroboration).
Without Participial Phrase	While courts do not condemn the use of photographs to aid the fact-finder in understanding a witness' testimony, photographs should not be resorted to where the witness can clearly convey the facts to the jury without their use. <u>Commonwealth v. Scaramuzzino</u>, 455 Pa. 378, 383 (1974) (**slides cumulative to pathologist's testimony**).
	The corroboration of an accomplice's testimony in cases of crimes for hire may consist primarily of the defendant's statements tending to connect the defendant to the crime. <u>Ex parte Bullock</u>, 770 So. 2d 1062, 1068 (Ala. 2000) (**arson for hire**); <u>Prewitt v. State</u>, 460 So. 2d 296 (Ala. Crim. App. 1984) (**murder for hire**).
	Recovery of damages for personal injuries to the fetus are allowed only where there is a subsequent live birth. <u>Witty v. Am. Gen. Capital Distribs., Inc.</u>, 697 S.W.2d 636, 639 (Tex. Ct. App. 1985) (**claims of emotional distress, mental anguish and loss of society**), <u>aff'd</u>, 727 S.W.2d 503, 506 (Tex. 1987).

☞ The final period goes outside the parenthetical at the end of the citation sentence. A period is included inside the parenthetical <u>only</u> if a full sentence is quoted.

☞ The parenthetical does not begin with a capital letter unless you are quoting a full sentence.

☞ Explanatory parentheticals precede subsequent history. See last example, above.

C. Combining Signals, Parentheticals, and/or Authorities

Signals and parenthetical explanations can be combined in a number of ways to concisely explain why an authority is being cited. Topics covered in this section are:

1. Combining separate signals into one signal;

2. Combining parentheticals and signals to explain the use of an authority;

3. String citing (using multiple authorities with a single signal); and

4. Using multiple signals for multiple authorities.

1. Combining Signals

- **Basic Rule:** The signal <u>e.g.,</u> can be combined with other signals to more precisely explain why an authority is cited. The combined signals are underlined [or italicized ♦] as one complete unit.

    Examples:

    <u>See</u> + <u>e.g.,</u>   ☞   <u>See e.g.,</u>

    <u>Compare</u> + <u>e.g.,</u>   ☞   <u>Compare e.g.,</u>

2. Combining Signals with Parentheticals   Rules 1.2 & 1.5

Some relationships between a signal, citation, and the proposition being cited, will not be clear without a parenthetical explanation. For that reason, *The Bluebook* encourages or strongly recommends the use of explanatory parentheticals with certain signals. The following table shows *The Bluebook*'s recommendations for using parenthetical explanations with signals.

Parentheticals Not Necessary (but may be helpful)	Parentheticals Encouraged	Parentheticals Strongly Recommended
[no signal]	See also	C.f.
E.g.	See generally	Compare
Contra		But c.f.
But see		

- **Basic Rule:** Include in parentheses at the end of a citation a phrase or sentence explaining the relevance of the proposition cited. Follow the rules for explanatory parentheticals in Part B. of this chapter.

Examples: Signals with Parentheticals

Parenthetical Not Necessary (but may be helpful)	Many cases hold that the criminal misuse of a firearm does not insulate the seller from liability arising out of a violation of similar provisions of the Gun Control Act. <u>K-Mart Enters. of Fla., Inc. v. Keller</u>, 439 So. 2d 283, 287 (Fla. Dist. Ct. App. 1983); <u>Franco v. Bunyard</u>, 547 S.W.2d 91 (Ark. 1977). **Contra** <u>Robinson v. Howard Bros. of Jackson, Inc.</u>, 372 So. 2d 1074 (Miss.1979).
Parenthetical Encouraged	For purposes of Rule 12(b)(6), the legislative history of an ordinance is an "adjunct to the ordinance" which may be considered by the court as a matter of law. <u>Anheuser-Busch v. Schmoke</u>, 63 F.3d 1305, 1312 (4th Cir. 1995). **See generally** 5A Charles A. Wright & Arthur R. Miller, <u>Federal Practice and Procedure</u> § 1357 (1990) **(in deciding Rule 12(b)(6) motions, courts may consider matters of public record)**.
Parenthetical Strongly Recommended	Individuals using wheelchairs may be mobile and functional in society but still disabled because of a substantial limitation on their ability to walk or run. <u>Finical v. Collections Unltd., Inc.</u>, 65 F. Supp. 2d 1032, 1039 (D. Az. 1999). **But c.f.** <u>EEOC v. Sears, Roebuck & Co.</u>, 233 F.3d 432, 439 (7th Cir. 2000) **(holding the use of a cane is a mitigating measure for the major life activity of walking)**.
See discussion of Multiple Signals for Multiple Authorities in subsection 4, below.	

3. String Citations   Rules 1.4 & B4.5

At times you may wish to list multiple authorities using a <u>single</u> signal (including "no signal"). This is commonly referred to as "string citation."

- **Basic Rule No. 1:** Authorities following a single signal (including "no signal") are separated by **semicolons** and are listed in a specific order. <u>See</u> Basic Rule No. 2.

- **Basic Rule No. 2:** Authorities are listed in strict order of hierarchy as established by Rule 1.4. Federal authorities precede state authorities, constitutions precede cases, etc. The most common authorities cited by practitioners are shown in the table below. Always consult *Bluebook* Rule 1.4 before ordering citations.

- **Exception to Basic Rule No. 2:** If one type of authority is "considerably more helpful or authoritative" than the other authorities listed, the more authoritative should be listed before other, less helpful, authorities.

  ☞ For example, if the law of a particular state controls your issue, a string cite to cases from several states should list the controlling state's cases first, even if they are "out of order" according to Rule 1.4.

Order of Multiple Authorities within String Citations

First	**Constitutions** by jurisdiction	1. Federal Constitution first; followed by 2. State constitutions, listed alphabetically by state.
Second	**Statutes** by jurisdiction	3. Federal statutes first, in progressive order of title and section number (e.g., 6 U.S.C. § 101 before 14 U.S.C. § 89); followed by 4. State statutes, listed alphabetically by state, then by progressive order of codification (e.g., § 12-222 before § 14-711).
Third	**Cases** by issuing court	5. U.S. Supreme Court 6. Federal courts of appeals 7. Federal district courts 8. Other federal courts (See *Bluebook* Rule 1.4(d)). ☞ All federal circuit courts of appeals are treated as one court; all federal district courts are treated as one court). 9. State high courts, listed alphabetically by state, then by rank (e.g., (a) Alaska high court, followed by intermediate court, then (b) Idaho high court, followed by intermediate court). **Cases from the SAME court are listed in REVERSE chronological order (i.e., newest first).**

This table shows only the three authorities most commonly cited by practitioners. <u>See</u> *Bluebook* Rule 1.4 for correct ordering of treaties, legislative materials, administrative and executive materials, international resolutions, records and briefs, and secondary materials.

Examples: Ordering Cases within String Citations

In a brief filed in an Illinois court:

Many courts have held that a claim for punitive damages in a tort action will survive the death of the injured person. <u>See e.g.</u>, **[1]** <u>Nat'l Bank of Bloomington v. Norfolk & W. R. Co.</u>, 383 N.E.2d 919 (**Ill.** 1978) (railroad accident); **[2]** <u>Froud v. Celotex Corp.</u>, 437 N.E.2d 910 (**Ill. App. Ct.** 1982) (asbestos-related diseases); **[3]** <u>Bancroft-Whitney Co. v. Glen,</u> 411 P.2d 92 (**Cal.** 1966) (breach of fiduciary duty); **[4]** <u>Evans v. Gibson</u>, 31 P.2d 389 (**Cal.** 1934) (fraud); **[5]** <u>Dunwoody v. Trapnell</u>, 120 **Cal.** Rptr. 859 (**Ct. App.** 1975) (medical malpractice); **[6]** <u>Black v. Gardner</u>, 320 N.W.2d 153 (**S.D.** 1982) (fraud and undue influence).

Note: The citations are numbered for discussion purposes only. Do not number citations in your string cites.

This excerpt cites cases from three states: Illinois [1]-[2], California [3]-[5], and South Dakota [6].

Illinois law controls the question before the court, thus Illinois cases [1] and [2] are cited first because they are "more authoritative," even though, alphabetically, they should follow the California cases.

California cases [3]-[5] are cited next, as California precedes South Dakota alphabetically. Cases [3] and [4] are both California Supreme Court cases (the state's highest court) and are listed in reverse chronological order. Case [5] is an appellate court case and is listed after the higher court cases.

Case [6] is listed last because South Dakota follows California alphabetically.

4. Multiple Signals for Multiple Authorities   Rules 1.3, 1.4, & B4.5

At times you may wish to list multiple authorities which offer different types of support for the proposition. This requires the use of multiple signals.

- **Basic Rule No. 1:** When using multiple SIGNALS to support one proposition, order the signals by TYPE of support, as shown in the following chart and in Rule 1.3. See chart below.

  ☞ In other words, to use the signals <u>see</u> and **but c.f.**, list the <u>see</u> signal and its authorities first because it is the first-ranked signal [Type (a)]. The <u>but c.f.</u> signal and its authorities would be listed second because it is lower ranked [Type (c)].

Order	Type of Signal <u>See</u> Rule 1.2	Rank within Signal Types
First	**Type (a):** Signals indicating support	1. [No signal] 4. See 2. E.g. 5. See also 3. Accord 6. C.f.
Second	**Type (b):** Signals indicating comparison	1. Compare
Third	**Type (c):** Signals indicating contradiction	1. Contra 2. But see 3. But c.f.
Fourth	**Type (d):** Signals indicating background material	1. See generally

- **Basic Rule No. 2:** Following each **signal**, order multiple citations to authority as described in *Bluebook* Rule 1.4, and illustrated in section C.3, above (string citations). Separate multiple citations following a single signal with **semicolons.**

  ☞ In other words, if a *signal* is followed by more than one authority, create a string citation for that signal.

- **Basic Rule No. 3:** Separate signals and their authorities of the SAME TYPE by semicolons. Separate DIFFERENT TYPES of signal and their authorities from other TYPES of signals and their authorities by **periods.**

  ☞ In other words, each *type* of signal (together with its authorities) is in it its own citation sentence, starting with a capital letter and ending in a period. Each new *type* of signal that is added begins a new citation sentence.

☞ Look carefully at how the signals and authorities are strung together in the examples below. Pay close attention to the punctuation that separate each signal type.

Examples: Multiple Signals with Multiple Authorities

Parking vehicles on a right of way may constitute the misuse of an easement for ingress and egress. See Keeler v. Haky, 325 P.2d 648, 653 (Cal. App. Ct. 1958) (using an alleyway for parking automobiles); Mad River Secs., Inc. v. Felman, 112 N.E.2d 646, 648 (Ohio 1953) (one owner's use of a private alley as a parking lot rendered it unusable for access by the adjoining owner); Cleveland v. Clifford, 698 N.E.2d 1045 (Ohio App. Ct. 1997) (patrons permitted to park in a manner that interfered with the servient estate owner's shared use of the driveway); see also Arcidi v. Town of Rye, 846 A.2d 535 (N.H. 2004) (easement providing secondary access). But see Jordan v. Worthen, 68 Cal. App. 3d 310 (1977) (burden on servient estate not unreasonable); Hill v. Allan, 259 Cal. App. 2d 470 (1968) (dominant estate's use was foreseeable).

Signal: See. This signal type (showing support) and its authorities are listed first, per Rule 1.3. Three authorities accompany this signal.

☞ 1. The California case is listed first because California comes alphabetically before Ohio.

☞ 2. Ohio cases are listed next, beginning with the Mad River case which is from Ohio's highest court.

☞ 3. The second Ohio case, Cleveland, is listed after the Ohio Supreme Court case as it is from a lower appellate court.

☞ **New signal: See also.** Because this is the SAME TYPE of signal as see (showing support), it is separated by a **semicolon**. **See also** is a lower-ranked signal type and follows the higher-ranked **see**.

☞ **New signal: But see.** Because this is the DIFFERENT TYPE of signal (showing contradiction), and is lower ranked, it is last and is separated from the prior signal by a **period**.

The two accompanying authorities [Jordan and Hill] are both California cases and are from the same level of court (appellate). Put in reverse chronological order.

Signals and Parentheticals Are Not a Substitute for Analysis!

It is easy to abuse both signals and parentheticals. While they are useful tools, writers should be wary of misuse. Do not substitute signals or parentheticals for an actual analysis of the cited authorities. Do not slap a signal such as "<u>see generally</u>" in front of a citation and convince yourself that the signal substitutes for explaining the relevant case law. Use explanatory parentheticals only for information that is simple and not an important part of your discussion or argument. If the material is important to the issue, always explain it in the text.

9 Quotations

Bluebook **Rules 5** and **B12** control the style for quotations in legal documents. This chapter discusses the following:

A. The basic form of quotations;

B. Making minor alterations to quotations; and

C. Omitting portions of quoted material.

A. Form of Quotations   Rule 5.1 & B12

- **Basic Rule:** Count the number of words in the quoted passage. If the quoted passage contains:

  1. **50 words or more**, use a block quotation, following the rules described in Part A.1., below.

  2. **49 or fewer** words, incorporate the quoted material directly into your text sentence or paragraph, following the rules described in Part A.2., below.

1. Block Quotations   Rules 5.1(a) & B12

- **Basic Rule:** Block quotations, used for quotations of 50 or more words, are:

  1. Single spaced;

  2. Fully justified;

  3. Indented left and right; with

  4. **No** quotation marks; and are

  5. Followed by a citation to the source of the quote placed at the **left margin** of the paper (not part of the block quote itself), leaving one blank line between the end of the block quotation and the citation.

2. Short Quotations   Rule 5.1(b)

- **Basic Rule:** Shorter passages of 49 or fewer words are incorporated into the text of the document as follows:

  1. The passage must be included within quotation marks;

  2. With no changes in format (e.g., no indentations or change of line spacing); and are

  3. Followed immediately by a citation to the source of the quote.

Examples: Quotations

50 Words or More – Rule 5.1(a)	49 Words or Less – Rule 5.1(b)
There are just a few simple rules for dealing with a block quote: Whenever you have a quotation of fifty words or more, place the quoted text in a block quote. Block quotes are created by indenting both sides of the quoted material. When a block quote is used, **do not use quotation marks**. The block quote should be single spaced and right-justified. Place the citation for the quotation at the left hand margin, being sure to skip a line between the end of the block quote and the citation. Smith v. Jones, 555 P.2d 555, 556 (Ore. 2001).	When your quotation is less than fifty words, you must "incorporate the quote directly into your sentence," placing the quoted material within quotation marks. Smith v. Jones, 555 P.2d 555, 558 (Ore. 2001). When a quote is incorporated into a text sentence, commas and periods are "placed inside the ending quotation mark." Id. at 556. And always be sure to follow the quotation "with a pinpoint cite." Id. at 557.

B. Alterations   Rule 5.2

Sometimes it is necessary to make a slight change to a quotation so that it fits neatly into the structure of your sentence or paragraph, or to insert a word to help the reader better understand the quoted material.

- **Basic Rule:** All alterations, no matter how small, must be indicated by enclosing the altered material in brackets. To omit letters from a root word, or to change a plural to singular, use empty brackets. See examples below.

Examples: Altering Quotations

Original	Altered
"**A** final judgment on the merits of an action precludes the parties or their privies from re-litigating issues that were or could have been raised in that action." Federated Dep't Stores v. Moitie, 452 U.S. 394, 398 (1981).	The United States Supreme Court has held that **"[a]** final judgment on the merits of an action precludes the parties or their privies from relitigating issues that were or could have been raised in that action." Federated Dep't Stores v. Moitie, 452 U.S. 394, 398 (1981) ☞ The "a" has been changed from a capital to lower case. The change must be indicated by placing the "a" in brackets.
"**H**aving determined that **Melia** is not entitled to prevail under either theory upon which recovery was sought, we need not discuss the punitive damage issue raised by **Dillon.**" Melia v. Dillon Co., 18 Kan. App. 2d 5, 10 (1993).	The court concluded that **"[h]**aving determined that **[plaintiff]** is not entitled to prevail under either theory upon which recovery was sought, we need not discuss the punitive damage issue raised by **[defendant].**" Melia v. Dillon Co., 18 Kan. App. 2d 5, 10 (1993) ☞ Three changes have been made here: (1) capitalization, (2) substitution of the word plaintiff for one party's name; and (3) substitution of the word defendant for the other party.
The death of an insured from a gunshot wound sustained while the insured, as the aggressor, was attempting to take the pistol from another, is "caused by accidental means within the double indemnity **provisions** of the policy. Mohn v. Am. Cas. Co. of Reading, 326 A.2d 346, 349 (Pa. 1974)	The death of an insured from a gunshot wound sustained while the insured, as the aggressor, was attempting to take the pistol from another, is "caused by accidental means within the double indemnity **provision[ ]** of the policy." Mohn v. Am. Cas. Co. of Reading, 326 A.2d 346, 349 (Pa. 1974) ☞ The plural word "provisions" was changed to the singular "provision." Omission of a letter is indicated by empty brackets.

Do not overuse alterations because they tend to distract and slow down the reader. Instead of quoting with multiple alterations, try paraphrasing.

C. Omissions   Rule 5.3

Quotations can be shortened to omit unnecessary detail. Any omission must be indicated by the use of an ellipsis.

- **Basic Rule**: Use three periods (dots) <u>separated by spaces</u> to indicate information that has been omitted from a quotation, subject to the following rules:

    1. To omit material **preceding** the quoted material, simply add quotation marks at the start of your quote. Do not use an ellipsis.

        ☞ *Right:*   "Start quote with quote marks."

        ☞ *Wrong:*   ". . . Do not use leading ellipsis."

    2. To omit material **incorporated within** a quoted passage, insert an ellipsis.

    3. To omit material at the **end** of a quote which also ends your sentence, use an ellipsis PLUS the final punctuation for your sentence (e.g., four periods, or three periods and a question mark).

Examples: Omissions

Location of Omitted Material	Original	Quote with Omissions
1. Preceding Material	~~Under federal maritime law,~~ in exercising its in personam jurisdiction in maritime cases, a state may adopt such remedies as it sees fit so long as it does not make changes in the substantive law. <u>Moragne v. States Marine Lines, Inc.</u>, 398 U.S. 375, 402 (1970).	"[I]n exercising its in personam jurisdiction in maritime cases, a state may adopt such remedies as it sees fit so long as it does not make changes in the substantive law." <u>Moragne v. States Marine Lines, Inc.</u>, 398 U.S. 375, 402 (1970). ☞ Do not use leading ellipsis. Indicate change of case by brackets.
2. Incorporated Material	Under federal maritime law~~, in exercising its in personam jurisdiction in maritime cases,~~ a state may adopt such remedies as it sees fit so long as it does not make changes in the substantive law. <u>Moragne v. States Marine Lines, Inc.</u>, 398 U.S. 375, 402 (1970).	"Under federal maritime **law . . . a** state may adopt such remedies as it sees fit so long as it does not make changes in the substantive law." <u>Moragne v. States Marine Lines Inc.</u>, 398 U.S. 375, 402 (1970).

Examples: Omissions *continued*

Location of Omitted Material	Original	Quote with Omissions
3. Ending Material	Under federal maritime law, in exercising its in personam jurisdiction in maritime cases, a state may adopt such remedies as it sees fit ~~so long as it does not make changes in the substantive law~~. Moragne v. States Marine Lines, Inc., 398 U.S. 375, 402 (1970). ☞ But note that this omission leaves out an important qualification of the rule. The next sentence must clarify so it is not misleading.	"Under federal maritime law, in exercising its in personam jurisdiction in maritime cases, a state may adopt such remedies as it **sees fit . . . .**" Moragne v. States Marine Lines, Inc., 398 U.S. 375, 402 (1970). ☞ Include final punctuation when the quote ends your sentence (4 periods, not three).

Important Note

Notice in the examples in this guide and in *The Bluebook*, when indicating an omission from a quotation, there are spaces before, between, and after the periods in an ellipsis.

Wrong: "Under federal maritime law...a state may adopt such remedies as it sees fit...."

Right: "Under federal maritime law . . . a state may adopt such remedies as it sees fit . . . ."

10 Capitalization

Bluebook Rules 8 and B10.6 control the capitalization of words and parties' names in legal documents. This chapter discusses the following rules:

A. General capitalization rules; and

B. Capitalization in court documents.

A. General Capitalization Rules   Rule 8

- **Basic Rule No 1: Titles and Headings.** Capitalize all words in a heading or title of a document, EXCEPT any article, conjunction or preposition that is less than five letters, UNLESS it is the first word of a heading or title, or follows a colon. Rule 8(a).

  Examples:

    The Politicization **of the** Convention Against Torture.

    Positive Action **and** European Union Law **in the** Year 2000.

    Extraordinary Rendition: **A** Human Rights Analysis.

- **Basic Rule No. 2: Specific Persons/Groups.** Capitalize nouns that identify SPECIFIC persons, officials, groups, government offices or government bodies; do not capitalize when the noun is a general reference. Rule 8(b).

  Examples:

    The **President** spoke briefly.

    The various organizations' **presidents** met briefly.

    The **Congress** met in regular session.

    The **congressional committees** gave their reports.

- **Basic Rule No. 3: Exceptions.** Certain words when used in certain contexts should always be capitalized. <u>See</u> *Bluebook* Rule 8(b) and the chart on the next page.

Examples: Capitalized Words   Rule 8(b)

CAPITALIZE	UNDER THESE CIRCUMSTANCES	EXAMPLES
Act	When referring to a specific legislative act.	The proposed **Act** will ensure privacy. *but not:* Legislatures in several states passed similar **acts**.
Circuit	When used with a circuit's name or number.	The Eleventh **Circuit** held the opposite. *but not:* Two **circuits** held the opposite.
Code	When referring to a specific statutory code.	The Delaware **Code** bars the conduct. *but not:* Most states' **codes** require approval before proceeding.
Court	When naming any court in full, or when referring to the United States Supreme Court.	The Florida Supreme **Court** held the statute was ambiguous. *but not:* A **court** previously ruled against the plaintiff in a similar case.
Commonwealth	If part of the full name of a state.	The **Commonwealth** of Kentucky. *but not:* Whether a **commonwealth** can impose this form of tax is unclear.
Constitution	When referring to the United States Constitution or when naming any constitution in full.	The New Mexico **Constitution**. *but not:* All states have **constitutions**.
Federal	When the word it modifies is capitalized.	The **Federal** Reserve oversees the programs. *but not:* The **federal** authorities do not agree.
Judge, Justice	When giving the name of a specific judge or justice, or when referring to a Justice of the Supreme Court.	**Chief Justice** John G. Roberts, Jr. *but not:* The **judge** ruled quickly.
State	When it is the part of the full title of a state, if the word it modifies is capitalized, or the state is a party to the litigation.	The **State** of Iowa agreed to render aid. *but not:* Whether the **state** would agree was unclear.
Term	When referring to a Term of the United States Supreme Court.	The **Term** of the Court began yesterday. *but not:* It was the beginning of the senator's **term** in office.

> The chart on the previous page illustrates the Basic Rule only. There are additional require-
> ments. See examples and exceptions in *Bluebook* Rule 8.
>
> __See also__ the rules for capitalization in court documents in Rule B10.6, discussed in the next
> section of this guide.

B. Capitalization in Court Documents   Rule B10.6

- **Basic Rule:** In documents that will be submitted to a court, follow Rule 8 (discussed in Part A. of this chapter), plus Rule B10.6. The following words <u>may</u> need to be capitalized according to the rules described in detail below:

  1. The word "court";

  2. Words designating parties to a legal action; and

  3. The title of court documents.

1. Courts   Rule 10.6.1

- **Basic Rule:** In text sentences, do not capitalize the word court when referring to a court gen-erally. Always capitalize the word "court" when referring to any of the following:

  (a) The full name of a specific court;

  (b) The United States Supreme Court; and

  (c) The court that will be receiving the document.

Examples: Capitalization of "Court"

CAPITALIZATION RULE	EXAMPLES
(a) Full Name of Court	The **Fifth Circuit Court of Appeals** held similarly.
(b) United States Supreme Court	The **United States Supreme Court** recently held the statute was unconstitutional.
(c) Receiving Court	This **Court** should reconsider the Plaintiff's motion. ***but not:*** The **court** ruled in plaintiff's favor in <u>Smith v. Jones</u>. ☞ The word "court" in the second example refers to a different court than the one receiving the document.

2. Parties to a Legal Action   Rule B10.6.2

- **Basic Rule:** Capitalize any words referring to parties to <u>your</u> legal action. Do not capitalize party designations in other legal actions (e.g., parties in precedent cases).

Examples: Capitalization of Parties' Names

Capitalize parties to YOUR legal action. This includes designations such as: • Plaintiff and Defendant • Appellant and Appellee • Petitioner and Respondent • Moving Party or Opposing Party	The **Respondent** failed to timely file any reply. The **Plaintiff** in our case testified that the **Defendant** was talking on his cell phone at the time of the accident.
Do not capitalize parties who are part of ANOTHER legal action. This includes parties to precedent cases.	In the <u>Sheffield</u> case, the **defendant** was similarly talking on his cell phone at the time he struck the **plaintiff's** car.

3. Titles of Court Documents   Rule B10.6.3

- **Basic Rule:** Capitalize the full or shortened titles of documents prepared in connection with <u>your</u> legal action. Do not capitalize generic names of court documents filed in your case, or court documents filed in other cases (e.g., precedent cases).

Examples: Capitalization of Court Document Titles

Titles of documents filed in YOUR action.	The Plaintiff's **Motion for Summary Judgment** should be denied.
Titles of documents filed in ANOTHER action.	The plaintiff's **motion for summary judgment** was denied in <u>Tatum</u>.
Generic reference to document.	In our case, the Plaintiff's and Defendant's various **motions** will be heard concurrently.

11 Numbers, Numerals, and Symbols

Bluebook **Rule 6.2** controls how numbers and numerals, including ordinals, are written in documents, and provides rules for inclusion of symbols in textual sentences. This chapter discusses the following:

A. When to spell out numbers or use numerals;

B. Ordinals; and

C. Use of section, paragraph and percent symbols, and dollar signs.

A. Numbers and Numerals   Rule 6.2(a)

- **Basic Rule No. 1:** Spell out the numbers zero to ninety-nine in textual sentences. Use numerals for numbers 100 and larger.

  - **Exception No. 1:** Spell out numbers in the following situations:

    (a) Numbers that begin sentences; and

    (b) Round numbers.

  - **Exception No. 2:** Use numerals in the following situations:

    (a) Numbers in a series that includes numbers both greater and less than 100;

    (b) Numbers that include decimals; and

    (c) Numbers that include repeated percentages or dollar amounts.

Examples: Numbers and Numerals

Basic Rule 1	Numbers zero to ninety-nine	Several witnesses, including **three** eye witnesses, testified at the trial.
Basic Rule 1	Numbers 100 and larger	Organizers said **175** people attended the meeting.
Exception 1(a)	Numbers that begin sentences	**Two hundred twenty** people attended the rally.
Exception 1(b)	Round numbers	A **thousand** replies were received.

chart continues on next page

Examples: Numbers and Numerals *continued*

Exception 2(a)	Numbers in a series	The police detained **55**, arrested **17**, and interviewed **135** others.
Exception 2(b)	Decimals	The plaintiff's temperature was **99.5** before she was given medication.
Exception 2(c)	Multiple percentages and dollar amounts	The fee will be discounted **25%** if payment is received within ten days, **20%** if payment is received within twenty days, and **10%** for payment within thirty days. Thus, if payment is made within ten days, deduct **$25**, within twenty days, deduct **$20**, and within thirty days, deduct **$10**.

- **Basic Rule No. 2: Commas.** For numbers FIVE digits or larger, use commas to separate thousands. DO NOT use a comma in numbers of FOUR digits. Rule 6.2(a)(vii).

Examples: Commas in Numerals   Rule 6.2

Basic Rule 2	**Numbers with five or more digits**	55,324
Basic Rule 2	**Numbers with 4 digits**	3966

B. Ordinals   Rule 6.2(b)

- **Basic Rule:** <u>In textual sentences</u> where a numeral is necessary, use "2nd" and "3rd." Do not use superscript.

  ☞ This applies only to ordinals in textual sentences and NOT CITATIONS. In citations, use "2d" and "3d."

Examples: Ordinals

Textual Sentences	The 102**nd** annual meeting was held.
	The 103**rd** Congress met in extraordinary session.
	☞ **Do not use superscript.** ☞ 102**nd**
Citations	N.E.2**d**
	103**d** Cong.

C. Symbols   Rules 6.2(c)-(d)

- **Basic Rule 1: Section and Paragraph Symbols.** Spell out the words "section" and "paragraph" in textual sentences, except when referring to sections of the United States Code. In citations sentences, use section [§] or paragraph [¶] symbols. Insert one space between the symbol and the numeral.

- **Basic Rule 2: Dollar Signs and Percent Symbols.** Spell out the words "dollar" and "percent" whenever numbers are spelled out. Use the symbols for dollars [$] and percent [%] whenever numerals are used. DO NOT insert a space between the symbol and the numeral.

  ☞ See discussion of when to spell out numbers in Part A. of this chapter.

Examples: Symbols

Section in textual sentence	The issue was addressed in **section 122** of the document.
Paragraph in textual sentence	The issue was addressed in **paragraph 122**.
Section in citation sentence	The act was a crime. **§ 15.3.14.**
Paragraph in citation sentence	The witness testified to the event. (Doe Aff. **¶ 24.**)
Dollars with spelled-out number	The price was **ten dollars**.
Dollars with numerals	The price was **$250**.
Percent with spelled-out number	The passage rate for the exam was **seventy-five percent**.
Percent with numerals	The price rose **150%**.
Beginning of a sentence	**One hundred fifty percent** price increases occurred.

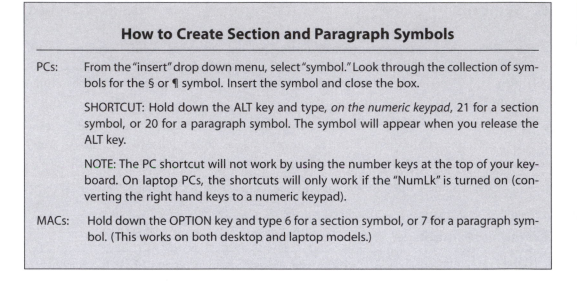

How to Create Section and Paragraph Symbols

PCs: From the "insert" drop down menu, select "symbol." Look through the collection of symbols for the § or ¶ symbol. Insert the symbol and close the box.

         SHORTCUT: Hold down the ALT key and type, *on the numeric keypad*, 21 for a section symbol, or 20 for a paragraph symbol. The symbol will appear when you release the ALT key.

         NOTE: The PC shortcut will not work by using the number keys at the top of your keyboard. On laptop PCs, the shortcuts will only work if the "NumLk" is turned on (converting the right hand keys to a numeric keypad).

MACs: Hold down the OPTION key and type 6 for a section symbol, or 7 for a paragraph symbol. (This works on both desktop and laptop models.)

Appendix: Citing Cases from On-Line Sources

Court of Appeals of Georgia.

FITZGERALD

v.

CAPLAN et al.

No. 75108.

> **Mark the first cite with one asterisk, mark the second case with two asterisks.** ☞

* **

184 Ga. App. 567, 362 S.E.2d 103

Oct. 5, 1987.

Rehearing Denied Oct. 19, 1987.
Certiorari Denied Nov. 19, 1987.

**104 Joseph B. Bergen, Frederick S. Bergen, Savannah, for appellant.

William P. Franklin, Jr., Wendy W. Williamson, Savannah, for appellees.

*567 BANKE, Presiding Judge.

This is an appeal by the plaintiff from a grant of summary judgment to the defendants in an action to recover for alleged medical malpractice and intentional infliction of emotional distress.

The evidence, construed most favorably towards the plaintiff as respondent on motion for summary judgment, may be summarized as follows. Defendant Gerald E. Caplan, M.D., acting as a member and agent of defendant Radiology Associates, P.A., performed a series of radiological tests on the plaintiff for the purpose of investigating the cause of abdominal pains that she was experiencing. The tests were performed at the request of another physician who was responsible for the actual treatment of the plaintiff and who is not a party to this litigation. One of the possible diagnoses being investigated was cancer.

The procedures performed by Dr. Caplan revealed that a portion of the plaintiff's pancreas was abnormally enlarged, confirming the possibility of cancer but warranting no definite diagnosis in this regard. In his report to the plaintiff's treating physician, Dr. Caplan wrote: "Close follow-up evaluation of the uncinate of the head of the pancreas is recommended although hopefully the change seen is not a manifestation of a neoplasm." In preparing an insurance claim form for submission to the plaintiff's medical insurance carrier, however, Dr. Caplan inserted or caused to be inserted in the space designated, "Diagnosis of nature of illness or injury," the following language: "157.9 Pancreas: Determine Extent of Malignancy." Dr. Caplan chose this language in an effort to fit the plaintiff's insurance claim into one of the pre-ordained diagnostic categories considered compensable by her insurance carrier, and thereby to minimize the possibility that the claim would be rejected.

A copy of the insurance claim form subsequently came into the hands of the plaintiff, who, upon reading it, was led to believe that she had been diagnosed as having cancer.

She immediately telephoned Dr. Caplan's office to verify this and was assured by his staff that the language in question had been used solely to expedite payment of her insurance claim. She was additionally informed that only her treating physician was in a position to discuss her final diagnosis with her. The plaintiff did in fact discuss the results of her radiographic tests with her treating physician **105 and was assured by him that she did not have cancer; however, the fear and concern which she had experienced upon reading the insurance form nevertheless did not abate.

> Note the page change for the S.E.2d reporter, above, identified by two asterisks, and the page change for the Georgia Appeals Reports, identified below by one asterisk.

The plaintiff does not argue in this appeal that Dr. Caplan's conduct constituted medical malpractice; however, she does urge in her *568 brief that he may be held liable in tort for intentional infliction of emotional distress based on the "negligent misinformation" which he caused to be transmitted to her.

☞ **It is a contradiction in terms to base a claim for intentional infliction of emotional distress on mere "negligent misinformation."** A cause of action for intentional infliction of emotional distress must be predicated on misconduct of an outrageous or egregious nature, which is "so terrifying or insulting as naturally to humiliate, embarrass or frighten the plaintiff." *Ga. Power Co. v. Johnson*, 155 Ga. App. 862, 863, 274 S.E.2d 17 (1980). [FN1] Clearly, Dr. Caplan's conduct in this case does not fall into this category. Indeed, it borders on the ridiculous to suggest that it was his intention to cause the plaintiff emotional distress or that he was engaged in some nefarious scheme to make money at the expense of her mental and emotional well being. Quite obviously, Dr. Caplan had no intention of terrorizing, harassing, or insulting the plaintiff but sought merely to avoid problems with her health insurance carrier, for her benefit as well as his own.

FN1. See, e.g., *American Fin. & Loan Corp. v. Coots*, 105 Ga.App. 849, 125 S.E.2d 689 (1962) (recovery authorized against bill collector who terrorized plaintiff and his family at gunpoint); *Delta Fin. Co. v. Ganakas*, 93 Ga.App. 297, 91 S.E.2d 383 (1956) (recovery allowed against defendant whose agent threatened small child with arrest in attempt to repossess her parents' television set); and *Stephens v. Waits*, 53 Ga.App. 44, 184 S.E. 781 (1936) (recovery allowed against defendants who physically intimidated plaintiffs as they were attempting to bury family member).

The cases relied upon by the plaintiff are quite distinguishable from the case before us and provide no support whatever for a recovery in this case. In *Greer v. Medders,* 176 Ga.App. 408, 336 S.E.2d 328 (1985), recovery was authorized against a physician who had verbally abused and insulted a patient and the patient's wife as the patient lay in a hospital bed attempting to recover from recent surgery. In *Chuy v. Philadelphia Eagles Football Club,* 595 F.2d 1265 (3rd Cir.1979), a case

which is not, in any event, binding on this court, the defendant physician inexplicably made a false announcement to the press that the plaintiff, a professional football player, was suffering from a fatal disease, knowing such was not the case. Although in *Stafford v. Neurological Med., Inc.,* 811 F.2d 470 (8th Cir.1987), the defendant physician's alleged misconduct was virtually identical to that alleged in the present case, the patient there did not merely suffer emotional distress as a result of the physician's misstatement on the insurance form, she committed suicide. Consequently, the plaintiff there was not limited to a recovery for intentional infliction of emotional distress but was authorized to recover on the basis of mere negligence.

Judgment affirmed.

Index of *Bluebook* Rules

Subject Index

NOTES

NOTES